W9-APE-825

# Robert Ballard

## The People to Know Series

**Neil Armstrong**
*The First Man on the Moon*
0-89490-828-6

**Isaac Asimov**
*Master of Science Fiction*
0-7660-1031-7

**Robert Ballard**
*Oceanographer Who Discovered the* Titanic
0-7660-1147-X

**Willa Cather**
*Writer of the Prairie*
0-89490-980-0

**Bill Clinton**
*United States President*
0-89490-437-X

**Hillary Rodham Clinton**
*Activist First Lady*
0-89490-583-X

**Bill Cosby**
*Actor and Comedian*
0-89490-548-1

**Walt Disney**
*Creator of Mickey Mouse*
0-89490-694-1

**Bob Dole**
*Legendary Senator*
0-89490-825-1

**Marian Wright Edelman**
*Fighting for Children's Rights*
0-89490-623-2

**Bill Gates**
*Billionaire Computer Genius*
0-89490-824-3

**Jane Goodall**
*Protector of Chimpanzees*
0-89490-827-8

**Al Gore**
*Leader for the New Millennium*
0-7660-1232-8

**Tipper Gore**
*Activist, Author, Photographer*
0-7660-1142-9

**Ernest Hemingway**
*Writer and Adventurer*
0-89490-979-7

**Ron Howard**
*Child Star & Hollywood Director*
0-89490-981-9

**John F. Kennedy**
*President of the New Frontier*
0-89490-693-3

**John Lennon**
*The Beatles and Beyond*
0-89490-702-6

**Maya Lin**
*Architect and Artist*
0-89490-499-X

**Jack London**
*A Writer's Adventurous Life*
0-7660-1144-5

**Barbara McClintock**
*Nobel Prize Geneticist*
0-89490-983-5

**Christopher Reeve**
*Hollywood's Man of Courage*
0-7660-1149-6

**Ann Richards**
*Politician, Feminist, Survivor*
0-89490-497-3

**Sally Ride**
*First American Woman in Space*
0-89490-829-4

**Will Rogers**
*Cowboy Philosopher*
0-89490-695-X

**Franklin D. Roosevelt**
*The Four-Term President*
0-89490-696-8

**Steven Spielberg**
*Hollywood Filmmaker*
0-89490-697-6

**Martha Stewart**
*Successful Businesswoman*
0-89490-984-3

**Amy Tan**
*Author of* The Joy Luck Club
0-89490-699-2

**Alice Walker**
*Author of* The Color Purple
0-89490-620-8

**Simon Wiesenthal**
*Tracking Down Nazi Criminals*
0-89490-830-8

**Frank Lloyd Wright**
*Visionary Architect*
0-7660-1032-5

# Robert Ballard

## *Oceanographer Who Discovered the* Titanic

*Christine M. Hill*

**Enslow Publishers, Inc.**
40 Industrial Road
Box 398
Berkeley Heights, NJ 07922
USA

PO Box 38
Aldershot
Hants GU12 6BP
UK

http://www.enslow.com

*For Leah*



**Library of Congress Cataloging-in-Publication Data**

Hill, Christine M.
Robert Ballard : oceanographer who discovered the Titanic / Christine M. Hill.
p. cm. — (People to know)
Includes bibliographical references and index.
Summary: A biography which covers the life and professional work of the man whose numerous missions to study the ocean floor led to the discovery of the wreck of the Titanic.
ISBN 0-7660-1147-X
1. Ballard, Robert D. 2. Titanic (Steamship)—History—Juvenile literature. 3. Shipwrecks—North Atlantic Ocean—History—Juvenile literature. 4. Oceanographers—United States—Biography—Juvenile literature. 5. Explorers—United States—Biography—Juvenile literature. [1. Ballard, Robert D. 2. Oceanographers. 3. Titanic (Steamship) 4. Shipwrecks.] I. Title. II. Series.
GC30.B35H55 1999
551.46'0092—dc21
[B] 98-54437
CIP
AC

Printed in the United States of America

10 9 8 7 6 5 4 3 2 1

**To Our Readers:**
All Internet addresses in this book were active and appropriate when we went to press. Any comments or suggestions can be sent by e-mail to Comments@enslow.com or to the address on the back cover.

Every effort has been made to locate all copyright holders of material used in this book. If any errors or omissions have occurred, corrections will be made in future editions of this book.

**Illustration Credits:** © Corel Corporation, pp. 18, 25; Enslow Publishers, Inc., p. 37; John Donnelly, Woods Hole Oceanographic Institution, p. 45; Martha Fenoglio, p. 83; Mystic Marinelife Aquarium, p. 104; National Archives, p. 107; Odyssey, Inc., pp. 95, 97; Reproduced from the Collections of the Library of Congress, pp. 9, 59; Rod Catanach, Woods Hole Oceanographic Institution, p. 28, 41; Woods Hole Oceanographic Institution, pp. 13, 35, 50, 73, 76.

**Cover Illustration:** Odyssey, Inc.

# Contents

## *Acknowledgment*

The author wishes to thank Dr. Robert Ballard for reading the manuscript.

# *Titanic* Found

April 10, 1912. The largest moving object ever made by man, the Royal Mail Steamer *Titanic*, stands at the dock in Southampton, England. At ten in the morning, boarding begins. People and luggage crowd the pier.

Three gangways stand side by side. The first-class gangway is reserved for the wealthy, boarding with their servants and possessions, even automobiles. A band plays at a reception to welcome them aboard.

The second-class gangway accommodates the middle-class passengers. Until departure, they are free to explore the ship, even the first-class areas. Twelve-year-old Ruth Becker pushes her baby brother along the deck in a carriage. Teacher Lawrence

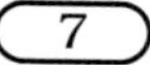

Beesley inspects the fully furnished gymnasium, where he looks forward to exercising.[1]

The third-class gangway swarms with passengers carrying their own bundles. They are mostly working people, emigrating to North America to seek their fortunes.

At noon, the gangways are withdrawn. Citizens of Southampton, who have turned out to watch, run along the dock, keeping pace with the great liner as it pulls away. Gaily waving passengers line the rails and peer from portholes.

Despite the festive atmosphere, Ruth Becker's mother is nervous. She quizzes an officer about the safety of the ship. There is nothing to worry about, he tells her. The *Titanic*'s watertight compartments would keep the ship floating. Many people aboard repeat the popular belief that the *Titanic* is unsinkable.[2]

Five days later, the *Titanic* will strike an iceberg and sink. Ruth Becker and her family and Lawrence Beesley will live to tell their stories. A total of 1,517 passengers, however, will perish. Then, for more than seventy years, the *Titanic*'s resting place will remain a mystery.

♦ ♦ ♦

People dreamed of seeing the fabled ship once more. One of those dreamers was Robert Ballard, head of the Deep Submergence Laboratory of the Woods Hole Oceanographic Institution in Massachusetts. Ballard, a renowned marine geologist and explorer, helped make some of this century's most important scientific

The World.

"Circulation Books Open to All."

VOL. LII. NO. 18,501. NEW YORK, TUESDAY, APRIL 16, 1912.

# GREAT TITANIC SINKS; MORE THAN 1,500 LOST; 866 WOMEN AND CHILDREN KNOWN TO BE SAVED; SCORES OF NOTABLES NOT ACCOUNTED FOR

THE LOST LINER, HER POSITION AND THAT OF OTHER SHIPS WHEN SHE HIT ICEBERG



## White Star Official Admits the Greatest Disaster in Marine History — J. J. Astor Rumored Lost, but Bride Saved — Text of Olympic's Fateful Message—Partial List Is Received.

### HOPE THAT MANY WILL BE FOUND ON WRECKAGE.

Virginian and Parisian Reach Scene Too Late—They Are Joined by Other Steamers, Which Find Only Debris—Capt. Smith Believed to Have Gone Down with Ship—The Saved Suffer Severely from Exposure, After Floating in the Lifeboats for Eight Hours.

More than fifteen hundred souls, men, women and children, were lost, it is feared, in the wreck of the White Star liner Titanic, latest and greatest ship of the seas, which collided with an iceberg at 10.25 P. M. Sunday night and sank off the Banks of Newfoundland at 2.20 A. M. yesterday, less than four hours after she had struck.

Capt. Haddock of the Olympic sent this despatch by wireless to the White Star line last evening:

"Carpathia reached Titanic position at daybreak. Found boats and wreckage only. Titanic sank about 2.20 A. M., in 41.46 North, 50.14 West. All her boats accounted for, containing about 675 souls saved, crew and passengers included. Nearly all saved women and children. Leyland liner Californian remained and searching exact position of disaster. LOSS LIKELY TOTAL 1,800 SOULS."

The exact text of this despatch was closely guarded until after midnight by Vice-President Franklin of the White Star line, who received it at 7 o'clock. It gave the first definite news of the sinking of the Titanic and of the great loss of life.

But it is believed that the words "loss likely total 1,800 souls" is an error due to the ignorance of Capt. Haddock and the rescued passengers of the total number of persons aboard.

There were, according to the ship's manifest, 325 first cabin, 285 second cabin, and 710 steerage, a total of 1,320 passengers, and a crew of 860. This would make 2,180 persons aboard and some late comers not on the passenger lists are believed to have brought the total up to 2,200. Deducting 675 from this, the lost would only number 1,505, which Mr. Franklin believes to be correct.

A wireless despatch from the Olympic was picked up by a Boston operator late last night, in which it was stated that the Carpathia was on her way to New York with 866 passengers rescued from the Titanic. The rescued, the despatch read, were mostly women and children, and the despatch concluded:

"Grave fears are felt for the safety of the balance of the passengers and crew."

The disparity between this number of rescued, 866, and the 675 mentioned in Capt. Haddock's despatch to the White Star line was explained on the theory that the Carpathia might have picked up some more passengers in lifeboats after the Olympic had sent her first message to the White Star line. Nothing to confirm this, however, was obtainable at the local offices of the line.

Vice-President Franklin of the White Star line admitted at 11 o'clock last night there seemed to be no doubt that at least 675, mostly women and children, of the 2,200 aboard the Titanic, had been rescued. These are aboard the Cunard liner Carpathia, which is hastening to New York. Said Mr. Franklin:

"The fact that Capt. Haddock of the Olympic (from whom came the news of the Titanic's loss) did not report the whereabouts of any other passengers than those upon the Carpathia discourages the hope that the Parisian or the Virginian of the Allan line, which went to the Titanic's assistance, saved any of the other passengers."

The disaster is the worst in marine history. Among those aboard the Titanic, making her maiden trip from Southampton to New York, were many men and women prominent in society, the arts, professions and in business.

Col. John Jacob Astor was a passenger, with his bride, nee Force. When Vincent Astor, the Colonel's son, called at the White Star offices last night and in tearful tones asked for news of his father, a rumor spread with lightninglike rapidity that Col. Astor had been drowned and Mrs. Astor saved. This could not be confirmed from any source.

Other notable men aboard the Titanic were Major Archibald Butt, Military Aide to President Taft; Charles M. Hays, president of the Grand Trunk Pacific Railroad, with his family; William T. Stead, of the London Review of Reviews; Benjamin Guggenheim, of the mining brotherhood; G. D. Widener, of Philadelphia; F. D. Millet, the noted artist; Mr. and Mrs. Isidor Straus, J. Thayer, vice-president of the Pennsylvania Railroad; J. Bruce Ismay, chairman of the White Star Line's board of directors; Henry B. Harris, theatrical manager; Col. Washington Roebling, the engineer, and scores of other well known men, with their wives in some cases, and their children.

Of the 325 first cabin passengers on the Titanic, 128 were women and 15 children. The second, 285 persons, included 79 women and 8 children, and in the steerage the complement of 710 was divided almost equally, it is believed, between women and men, with a small percentage of children.

The numbers are enough to indicate that if the women and children were saved, very few men could have survived the disaster, as there were almost enough women and children aboard to make up the total of 675 survivors.

Capt. E. J. Smith, of the Titanic, is believed to have gone to the bottom with his vessel.

It was announced last night at the offices of the White Star Line that those rescued had been picked up by the Carpathia, which reached the scene of the wreck about 10 o'clock, eight hours after the Titanic had sunk. The survivors were roaming about, in a small fleet of lifeboats, on the rolling waves and in the muggy weather of the Banks.

They had suffered severely through the night, and so far as the Olympic's captain, who got to the spot in the afternoon could ascertain, there were no other survivors.

It had been reported at first that many had been rescued by the Allan liner Virginian and the Parisian, but

## LIST OF THE KNOWN SAVED

CAPE RACE, N. F., April 16 (Tuesday, 2 A. M.)—Following is a partial list of the first-class passengers who were rescued from the Titanic:

APPLETON, Mrs. EDWARD W.
ABBOTT, Mrs. ROSE.
BURNS, Miss C. M.
CASSEBERE, Miss D. D.
CLARKE, Mrs. WILLIAM M.
CHIBINACO, Mrs. B.
CROSSBIE, Miss E. G.
CROSSBIE, Miss H. E.
SIPPACH, Miss JEAN.
HARRIS, Mrs. HENRY B. (wireless version Mrs. L. Y. B. Harris).
LEADER, Miss A. F.
LAVORY, Miss BERTHA.
LIVES, Mrs. ERNEST.
ROGERSON, Mrs. SUSAN P.
ROGERSON, Miss EMILY B.
ROGERSON, Mrs. ARTHUR.
ALLISON, Master, and nurse, Miss E. T. ANDREWS.
PANHART, Miss Ninette.
ALLEN, Miss E. W.
BISHOP, E. D., and Mrs. BISHOP.
BLANK, Mr. H.
BASSINA, Miss A.
BAXTER, Mrs. JAMES.
BAYTON, GEORGE A.
BONNELL, Miss C.
BROWN, Mrs. J. M.
BOWEN, Miss G. C.
HALVERSON, Mrs. ALEX.
HAYS, Miss MARGARET.
ISMAY, BRUCE.
KIMBERLEY, ED., and Mrs. KIMBERLEY.
KENTMAN, F. A.
KENCHEN, Miss EMILE.
LONGLEY, Miss G. F.
BECKWITH, R. L., and Mrs. BECKWITH.
WARNER, Mrs. F. M.
WILSON, Miss HELEN A.
WILLARD, Miss.
WICKS, Miss MARY.
WIDENER, Mrs. GEORGE D., and maid, Mrs. J. STEWART.
WOOLMER, H.
WARD, Miss ANNA.
WILLIAM, RICHARD M.
WHITE, Mrs. J. STEWART.
YOUNG, Miss MARIE.
POTTER, Mrs. THOMAS, Jr.
ROBERTS, Mrs. EDNA S.

The foregoing list was received by wireless at Cape Race station from the steamer Carpathia. In spelling and initials it does not correspond with the list as cabled from London to-day.

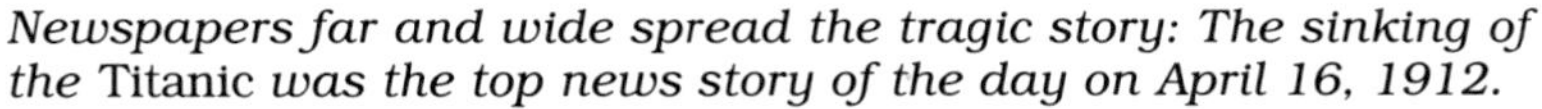

*Newspapers far and wide spread the tragic story: The sinking of the* Titanic *was the top news story of the day on April 16, 1912.*

discoveries. But his greatest desire was to find and explore the legendary wreck. He plotted and planned and patched together funding for his quest over many years. At last, he launched his expedition and began searching on July 5, 1985.

Now it was midnight, September 1, 1985. Only four days remained for Ballard and his team of French and American scientists to reach their goal. Their research vessel *Knorr* was chartered for another expedition.

Ballard had read eyewitness accounts of the *Titanic*'s sinking and the logbooks of nearby vessels. He had studied the wind and current conditions of that night. Using these data, he targeted a one-hundred-square-mile area where he predicted the *Titanic* lay.

With sound waves and underwater video, his team scanned the ocean bottom. The camera sled, nicknamed *Argo*, hung from a twelve-hundred-foot cable. It tracked back and forth, back and forth, tracing lines on the seafloor. Scientists call it "mowing the lawn."[3] The search had been unsuccessful. *Argo*'s camera saw only mile upon mile of mud and sand hills. Occasionally, a boulder or sea slug track would break the monotony.

The midnight shift began with the murmur of voices. The crew retiring for the night checked the latest data with their replacements. A concerned Ballard carefully instructed the navigator, Cathy Offinger, on the night's search strategy. He told her they would pass over a section missed early in the search, a slice of bottom only one mile wide and five miles long.[4]

Ballard waited for a superstitious crew member to make his nightly prediction of when the ship would be found. "I hoped against hope that tonight he would be right," Ballard wrote.[5]

Printers clacked, sonar pinged. Someone popped a tape of sixties hits into the cassette player. Ballard lingered in the control room for a while. Finally, he slipped off to his cabin.

He lay in his bunk unable to sleep. He faced up to the possibility of defeat for the first time. He had never been defeated professionally. To clear his mind of worry, he decided to read a book.

Back in the control room, a yawning crew member asked, "What are we going to do to keep ourselves awake tonight?"[6] His colleague, Stu Harris, was strangely silent, staring at the video monitor.

"There's something," he said tentatively.[7]

With mounting excitement, the crew gathered around the monitor to see for themselves. Their voices rang out with each new image, some in awe, some hoarse with emotion.

"Wreckage!"

The screen showed rusty pipes and fittings, clearly old, clearly man-made. But how old were they? And were they from the *Titanic*?

"Bingo! Yeah!"

Past the metallic objects, mud reappeared. The crew began to doubt their senses and rewound the video.

"Did you find it?"

"Well, we got something."

Wreckage again filled the screen. *Argo* was crossing

the previously missed sliver of seafloor. Ballard's hunch had proved correct.

"Someone ought to go get Bob."

No one moved. They could not tear themselves away from the video monitor.

"Oh, I love it! I love it!"

"This is *it*!"[8]

Again, someone suggested that Ballard be called. The ship's cook, who had happened to drop by, ran to fetch him. Ballard threw a team jumpsuit over his pajamas. "I wore those pajamas for the next five days," he later confessed.[9]

Ballard flew down three flights of slippery deck. Meanwhile, a massive circular object appeared on the video monitor. Three round vents crowned it. The crew began to exclaim.

"That is big!"

"Look at it!"

There was a pause.

"The boiler!" a crew member croaked.

"Yes, yes . . . the boiler," others agreed.

"Fantastic . . . all *right*!" they whooped.

Ballard had required the crew to study the history and architecture of the great ship. There was no mistaking one of the *Titanic*'s twenty-nine distinctively designed boilers.

"Bob!" someone shouted.

Ballard entered the van.

"We got the boiler!"[10]

Ballard rewound and viewed the video. He saw that his dream had come true. Ballard and his team had found the *Titanic*. "The film crew was documenting this

*Robert Ballard, second from right, stands in front of the camera sled* Argo *with some other members of his* Titanic *expedition team in 1985. Their discovery of the* Titanic's *resting place on the ocean floor thrilled the world.*

historic event, and I knew I should have some fitting words to say. But words failed me," Ballard admitted.[11]

Ballard turned to his partner, Jean-Louis Michel of France. He clapped his moist-eyed friend on the shoulder. "It was not luck," Michel told him. "We earned it."[12]

Word of the discovery spread through the ship. Almost the entire expedition crew crowded into the control room.

"There was an immediate outpouring of excitement," Ballard recalled. "Bunch of kids . . . yelling and screaming and jumping up and down. Very unprofessional."[13]

Then someone looked at the clock. It showed almost 2:00 A.M. Years earlier the *Titanic* had slid beneath the Atlantic's frigid waters at 2:20 A.M.

"Then the whole force of actually being at the very spot where this tragedy had taken place [hit]. . . . Everyone just crashed."[14]

Ballard spoke to the crew. "In about twenty minutes," he said, "I'm going out on the fantail. If anyone wants to join me, they're welcome." He left the room. He needed to be alone.[15]

The crew found him, hat off, hair blowing in the wind, head bowed, hands on the stern rail, contemplating the sea. A calm ocean mirrored the stars, just as it had on April 15, 1912. Ballard called for a moment of silence. Then he said, "Thank you all. Now let's get back to work."[16]

# Boyhood by the Sea

Robert Ballard was born in Wichita, Kansas, on June 30, 1942. His ancestors had emigrated from England to America in the 1600s. Their pioneering spirit, which Robert Ballard inherited, pushed them westward to Kansas by the 1800s.

Ballard's grandfather was a law enforcement officer in Wichita in the 1920s. He was slain, along with two deputies, in a shoot-out. Ballard's father, Chester, was only five at the time. Seven years later, Chester's mother also died. The twelve-year-old orphan was sent to his great-uncle's ranch in Montana's beautiful Stillwater Valley. Young Chester spent his teens working as a cowboy.

Robert Ballard cherishes his western roots. "I've

got a good dose of cowboy in me: I mean a freer spirit. I haven't been broken," he says.[1] But Chester did not flourish as a cowpuncher. He remembered Montana's intense cold and being "the kid" passed from relative to relative.[2] Chester Ballard's intelligence became his ticket out of Montana. He got a job as a flight-test engineer.

Chester Ballard married Harriett May, whose German ancestors had arrived in the Midwest in the 1850s. Harriett and Chester Ballard had two sons: Richard, born in 1940, then Robert, two years later. Not long after Robert was born, the young couple settled in California's Mojave Desert at Muroc Air Force Base. Chester Ballard worked as a developer of the first supersonic jets. Among young Bob's first childhood memories were jets streaking across the sky and giant tortoises, coyotes, and rattlesnakes roaming the desert.

Chester Ballard often drove his sons to the beach on weekends. The two little boys loved running and playing in the sand, but they were afraid of the ocean. Their father patiently built sand castles with them week after week. Gradually, he started the castles closer and closer to the wet sand. The boys began to allow the waves to lap over their feet as they built. Finally, they plunged into the water unafraid. "Now look, fellas," Chester Ballard had to warn them, "people *can* go too far into the water."[3]

Bob was delighted to live near the ocean when the family moved to San Diego, California. In 1948, it was still a small city on the Pacific. "The ocean was a friend and an adventure to me," he says.[4] Bob spent hours walking the beaches and exploring tidal pools with his friends. "Every twelve hours the tidal pool changed—a different set of animals got trapped," he remembers. "So tidal pools were the microcosm that I was an explorer of. And I've never grown up. I mean I still have that childish desire to poke around."[5]

Bob's older brother, Dick, was an exceptional student like their father. Bob's grades were good but not outstanding. "I couldn't out-think them, especially in math, so I had to out-talk them," Ballard says.[6] He specialized in trying to make his father laugh. The family agreed that Bob took after his mother's father, Jack May, a master talker and salesman. In the coming years, Bob would use his sense of humor and persuasive abilities to sell others on his dreams.

Ballard's sister, Nancy, was born during the San Diego years. A birth defect that damaged the speech center of her brain left her unable to talk. The Ballards constantly sought better therapy and education for her. She grew up loving sports, particularly boating and fishing. Bob was her devoted protector. She inspired him. "How could I squander any opportunity if she never had one?" he asked.[7]

Chester Ballard continued to advance in the aerospace design industry. In 1953 the family moved again. Downey, California, a suburb of Los Angeles, was their new home. Huntington Beach, one of the Pacific Coast's top surfing spots, was nearby. Bob became an avid bodysurfer. "I feel like the creature from the Black Lagoon. I've got to keep my gills wet," he said.[8]

Bob was a skilled athlete. In high school he played

*"The ocean was a friend and an adventure to me," says Robert Ballard of his childhood years in San Diego, California. There he spent hours exploring the beaches.*

football, basketball, and tennis. He also took up scuba diving. These activities helped him carve out an identity distinct from his brilliant brother's. He dated and hung out at fast-food restaurants, like other teenagers.

Bob was also an avid reader. He devoured adventure stories set in the African wilds or in outer space. He read biographies of the explorers who became his heroes—Captain Cook, Admiral Byrd, and Admiral Peary. "I loved the story of Robinson Crusoe, walking the deserted beach finding treasures that had been washed up," he says.[9] He read and reread *A Night to Remember*, about the sinking of the *Titanic*. It captivated him almost as much as his favorite book, Jules Verne's *Twenty Thousand Leagues Under the Sea*. He identified strongly with Verne's hero, the rebel scientist Captain Nemo. Nemo traveled around the world underwater in his submarine, the *Nautilus*. "I'm still trying to be Captain Nemo," Ballard says.[10]

He wondered if this fascination could be turned into a career. Could he actually make a living studying the ocean? He confided his dream to his father. Chester Ballard's high-tech military work had brought him into contact with the head of the world-famous Scripps Institution of Oceanography in nearby La Jolla. Dr. Revelle of Scripps suggested that Bob apply for the 1959 National Science Foundation summer oceanography program. Bob did apply and was accepted.

After several weeks of research ashore, Bob cruised with the Scripps team along the Pacific Coast to the south. They gathered water samples, testing quality and temperature. Bob loved to take the most dangerous assignment. He stood in a container called a hero bucket, suspended from the side of the ship. Waves crashed over him as he attached sample bottles to a weighted line.

On the program's next expedition, the research vessel *Orca* cruised into a major hurricane off the northern California coast. Bob became so ill he could not eat. Another crew member fell from his bunk and broke his hip. The man was in great pain and needed medical attention. But the ship could not return to land in the storm. *Orca*'s captain radioed the U.S. Coast Guard to arrange an evacuation of the injured man. During the evacuation, both the Coast Guard cutter and the *Orca* were hit by a rogue wave. This towering monster, several waves combined, blasted the research ship. The wave shattered all of *Orca*'s windows and portholes, almost sinking it. When the storm subsided, the ship sputtered into the closest port for major repairs. The students were bused back to La Jolla.

A worried Chester Ballard waited for his son at the institution.[11] Would Bob be willing to continue in the program after his harrowing experience? Chester Ballard impatiently scanned the students as they stepped off the bus. Then he saw his son. "Wow! Absolutely incredible!" the boy exclaimed. "I've got to go out there again. Got to."[12]

3

# Young Scientist

A series of injuries marred Bob's senior year in high school. A concussion cut short his football season. Then torn ligaments and a broken ankle ended his basketball and tennis seasons. His grades were good enough, however, to give him a choice of colleges. He ruled out the University of California at Berkeley, where his brother was studying physics. Bob wanted his own identity in college. He remembered a geology professor from the university's Santa Barbara campus. He had met the professor on the *Orca* cruise. After visiting him at the beautiful seaside campus, Bob applied there and was accepted for the September 1960 freshman class.

Ballard threw himself eagerly into college life. He joined a fraternity and ran for student government.

He played varsity and intramural sports. He drilled in the Army Reserve Officers Training Corps (ROTC). This program prepared college students to be military officers.

He also challenged himself academically. He chose the physical sciences program. It required a student to major in both chemistry and geology. He minored in physics and math, as well. The program was so intense that students were expected to graduate in five years rather than four.

Yet Ballard never regretted it. "It was brutal," he remembers, "but I ended up with a very, very broad-based education. I'm able to follow my interests and sort of 'surf' . . . through science, and it's given me a great deal of freedom."[1]

Ballard's junior year was so hectic with activity that his grades suffered. Ballard realized he would need to buckle down to be admitted to graduate school. He worked much harder during his senior year. He also became engaged to be married. He decided to apply to the Scripps Institution of Oceanography for its doctoral program.

Scripps turned him down. It was Ballard's first real failure, a stunning blow. When his fiancée broke their engagement shortly after, Ballard reeled. "[It] threw me off course, sort of disoriented me for six or nine months," he remembered.[2] He spent the summer of 1964 studying business and accounting at the University of California at Los Angeles. He was unsure whether to continue in science.

His parents urged him not to give up on oceanography. Ballard spent his final semester at Santa

Barbara applying to every graduate oceanographic program he could think of. The University of Hawaii accepted him. He hopped on a plane to the islands as soon as he finished college in January 1965. It would be a fresh start.

Ballard needed a job to support his graduate studies. He heard about a position with the Oceanic Institute, not far from the university. The institute specialized in studying cetaceans—dolphins, porpoises, and whales. A trained-animal center and theater, Sea Life Park, helped support the institute's research.

When Ballard arrived for his interview, the head trainer handed him a swimsuit. She told him to jump into a nearby tank. Ballard saw several dark shapes in the bottom. Then he saw several sets of fins coming right at him. Years of scuba diving had given Ballard a healthy respect for sharks. He gulped, and—remembering that the institute studied marine mammals, not man-eaters—he stayed in the tank. Yes, they were dolphins, he realized.[3] Soon they swam close to him. They allowed him to rub their necks under the chin, just as they liked. The animals accepted him and Ballard had a job.

The head trainer quickly spotted Ballard's gift for gab. She put him before the audience at Sea Life Park. He sometimes performed as many as five shows a day. "I had to do a lot of acting and improvisation to keep them from being dull," he remembers.[4] This experience with public speaking would be valuable in later years.

The most important part of Ballard's work was cetacean training. The researchers trained some animals to do tricks. Others drilled for highly specialized naval research. In 1966, the acute intelligence of cetaceans was just beginning to be understood. "It would have been fairer to describe my work . . . as those clever animals training me," Ballard observes.[5]

Ballard undertook the training of an adolescent rough-toothed dolphin named Hou. The Navy needed her for a series of experiments on dolphin diving. "Training dolphins was very strange," Ballard says. "I will carry it with me for the rest of my life . . . [Hou] reached a point where love became the motivating tool in the training. Forget the fish, it was really affection and caring. I literally loved that animal like a human would love a human."[6]

When Hou was sent on her Navy mission, she resisted performing experiments in the open sea. Instead of swimming alongside the research vessel in her attached cage, she banged into the bars. She refused to perform more than a few dives. She seemed listless. The head researcher canceled the experiments when Hou developed a cold.

Back at the institute, Ballard climbed into Hou's tank to see what was the matter with her. The dolphin, who had been so devoted to him, butted him hard. Ballard believed Hou was angry with him for subjecting her to the training. He climbed out and quit his job. He never worked with dolphins again. To this day he speaks of his experiences with great sadness.[7]

In graduate school, Ballard remained in the Army Reserve. The reserves provide a pool of military people who can be called to active duty in case of a national emergency. While living in Hawaii, Ballard transferred from the Army Reserve to the Navy Reserve. The

*Ballard knows firsthand about the intelligence of dolphins. At the Oceanic Institute in Hawaii, he was hired to train dolphins. Really, though, it was "those clever animals training me," says Ballard.*

Vietnam War was raging in 1966. The United States was sending soldiers to fight in Vietnam to try to prevent the Communist government that ruled in the North from taking over the whole country. At this time, young American men were required by law to serve in the military. They could postpone their service as long as they pursued an education, however. Ballard obtained permission to do so.

Ballard also began dating a young woman whose apartment was across the street from his. Marjorie Hargas was working temporarily in a Honolulu flower shop. She had planned a brief stop in Hawaii to earn money to continue a trip around the world.

Then, in July, Ballard received an exciting job offer. North American Aviation wanted him to research manned deep-submersibles. These small submarines would be used for ocean exploration and commercial ventures. The company would pay for him to complete his Ph.D. studies at the University of Southern California. Only his deepening relationship with Marjorie Hargas tied him to Hawaii. Ballard proposed to her and she accepted. They married in California in July 1966.

Working for the Ocean Systems Group at North American Aviation was like "a dream come true," Ballard remembered.[8] But only a few months later, in early 1967, the Navy rudely awakened him from his dream. A naval officer appeared at his door with orders that he appear for active military duty. The Navy mistakenly believed that Ballard was still single and finished with school. It was too late to correct the error.

At least the Navy allowed Ballard to complete the semester. And the Navy would put his scientific skills to use. He was assigned to the Office of Naval Research in Boston, Massachusetts. His job would be to work with New England scientists who were doing research for the Navy.

Ballard and his wife drove cross-country in their Volkswagen Beetle. They taped their life savings of $1,000 to the bottom of the dashboard. After arriving during a March blizzard, Ballard could not help but think, "My life is ruined."[9]

A week later, the sun shone as spring arrived. Ensign Ballard reported to the Woods Hole Oceanographic Institution in Woods Hole, Massachusetts. The top oceanographic research center in the East, the institution is located on Vineyard Sound, at the edge of Cape Cod. It would become Ballard's scientific home for more than thirty years.

Ballard's eye promptly fell on the white tower of a bulbous, twenty-two-foot-long vessel moored in the institution's boat basin. It was *Alvin*, the most famous manned submersible in the world. Just the previous year, *Alvin* had gained fame when it found and retrieved a hydrogen bomb lost in the Mediterranean Sea. Ballard was intrigued by the sight of the sub.

Next, he called on the renowned geologist K. O. Emery. Dr. Emery took a personal interest in the young man. He insisted that Ballard must return to graduate school when his military service was over.[10] At that point, Ballard was skeptical. He would be in his late twenties by then. He might have a family to support. But Emery persisted. Ballard could continue

*Woods Hole Oceanographic Institution, Woods Hole, Massachusetts, in 1968. Ballard would work at this top research center for more than thirty years.*

his scientific studies by accompanying him on research cruises, he suggested.[11] "Maybe my life wasn't ruined after all," Ballard considered.[12]

The Ballards moved to an apartment south of Boston. Their first son, Todd, was born in July 1968. The young couple lived cheaply on Ballard's small naval salary. In his spare time, Ballard scuba dived with the Boston Sea Rovers. This is one of America's oldest diving clubs. Over steamed lobsters they had snatched from the bottom, the divers swapped stories around a blazing fire. They loved to talk about exploring underwater wrecks. Everyone agreed that the greatest of all was the *Titanic*. But it was an unobtainable prize, they believed. Even *Alvin* could only dive to less than half the depth of the ocean where the wreck was believed to lie.

For two years, Dr. Emery was as good as his word about teaching Ballard. When Ballard accompanied him on expeditions, Emery gave Ballard data to analyze on his own. Ballard was able to publish scientific papers while still in the Navy. During one cruise, he received an urgent call on the ship-to-shore radio. Fearing that something had happened to his year-old son, Ballard raced to the receiver. It was his naval commanding officer. The Navy was giving reserve officers a choice. Ballard could become a career officer or be released from duty. He had to decide right away.

He chose to resign from the Navy, though that left him without an income. The Woods Hole Oceanographic Institution quickly hired him to be its salesman. Ballard would persuade government agencies and research scientists to book time on *Alvin*.

Ballard bubbled over with ideas for funding sources, some practical, some far-fetched. The *Titanic*, he thought. "Find the *Titanic* with *Alvin*. Now that would really be a feat, the publicity would be terrific."[13]

Dr. Emery helped arrange Ballard's acceptance to the graduate geology program at the University of Rhode Island. With hard work, Ballard could complete the Ph.D. requirements in only a few years. The late sixties and early seventies were a period of intense activity for Ballard. He worked full-time, went to school full-time, did research, and spent months at sea. The Ballards' second son, Douglas, was born in October 1970. "[The boys] didn't see much of their dad during those exhausting graduate student years," Ballard admits. "Neither did Marjorie."[14]

During that period, *Alvin* underwent a refitting. Project TITANUS, funded by the U.S. Navy, gave *Alvin* a new personnel chamber. It was made of titanium, a rare metal, extraordinarily light and strong. The titanium chamber would protect divers from the deep ocean's extreme pressure. For the first time, *Alvin* would be able to dive to the average ocean depth of about twelve thousand feet.

When the Navy funding was approved, Ballard was at *Alvin* group headquarters. He immediately looked at an ocean wall map. His gaze focused on the mid-Atlantic, southeast of Newfoundland, Canada. At last *Alvin* was in range of the *Titanic*'s grave. Project TITANUS, titanium, *Titanic* . . . "I was struck by the closeness of those three words," he remembered.[15]

# Puzzle of the Continents

When Ballard began graduate school, professors still ridiculed the idea that continents could "drift." Alfred Wegener had proposed this idea in 1912. He had noticed, like many other people, that the continent shapes seemed to fit together like puzzle pieces. He wondered if they had gradually separated. Absurd, geologists responded, solid-rock continents cannot move.

Then sonar was developed during World War II. It measured sound waves as they traveled to and through the seafloor. Tests showed that the solid crust of the continents is as little as one hundred miles thick. Perhaps, scientists proposed, continents rode on movable plates over molten rock. Perhaps the plates holding the continents *had* separated over time.

Ballard believed in the theory of continental drift, now called plate tectonics. He decided to study the Appalachian Mountains for his Ph.D. Ballard theorized that he would find exactly the same kinds of rocks on land and under the ocean if they had once been joined. Dozens of times during 1971 and 1972, he dived in the Gulf of Maine, using *Alvin* to gather rock samples.

The French and American governments proposed a joint study. They planned to dive to the Mid-Atlantic Ridge, an underwater mountain range. There scientists would see with their own eyes if the North American and African plates were pulling apart. The Americans would dive in *Alvin*, the French in their own submersibles. The study was called Project FAMOUS, for French-American Mid-Ocean Undersea Study.

The French took to the sea with their bathyscaphe *Archimede*, a research submarine, in August 1973. Only one American scientist accompanied them: Robert Ballard. Even without his Ph.D. degree, he was the most accomplished deep-sea explorer in the world. *Archimede* resembled an underwater blimp. Far less maneuverable than *Alvin*, it traveled best up and down.

The French honored Ballard with a seat for the second descent of the project. On the morning of the dive, he awoke shaking with chills and fever. No sore throat, however, would keep him from this historic occasion. *Archimede*'s dark personnel compartment was crowded with three occupants. Ballard said not a word about his illness to the two French pilots. In any case, they spoke little of each other's language.

They descended to an underwater cliff in the rift valley. There, Ballard would observe and document seafloor spreading and underwater lava flows. A series of steps formed the cliff. The sub bounced down one step to the next, clumsily gathering samples.

Suddenly, the sub pitched forward, throwing the divers in a heap. The French muttered tensely to each other. Ballard felt the sub ascend. Its instruments showed that a problem in its electrical system caused the mission to abort. The pilots broke out wine, cheese, and bread to pass the time.

Then Ballard smelled it—the acrid fumes of an electrical fire. The pilots frantically shut down power. Ballard, already congested, struggled to breathe. The chief pilot grabbed three emergency oxygen masks. Ballard pulled his on, only to feel a fire in his lungs. He ripped it off. The chief pilot forced the mask back on. Ballard choked, nearly suffocating. Again he dragged off the mask. This time, both pilots, thinking he was panicking, struggled to replace it.

"I was not panicking. I was dying," Ballard remembered.[1] He ran a finger across his throat to signal that he was getting no air. After a moment's confusion, they understood and opened a valve. They had forgotten to turn on Ballard's oxygen tank. "Pardon," the chief pilot apologized.[2]

The French dives confirmed that forces deep in the earth were pulling the seafloor apart. Instead of one great crack, however, scientists saw many small parallel rifts. The farther they traveled from the valley center, the wider the rifts became.

Just before the next year's expedition, Ballard at last earned his Ph.D. degree. Now he was Dr. Ballard. His scientific credentials were established.

Twenty-four Americans joined the French for the next phase of Project FAMOUS in 1974. *Alvin* accompanied them. The sun sparkled on the waves for Ballard's plunge in *Alvin* on July 1, 1974. He wrote about the dive for *National Geographic* magazine. It would be the first of his many articles about science in the popular press. Ballard had a gift for communicating the complexity and excitement of science to the average person.

A giant elevator lowered *Alvin* partially into the water, Ballard wrote. He and volcanologist Jim Moore clambered through the hatch. They arranged their arms and legs in the compact personnel sphere. It measured only eighty inches in diameter and was packed with scientific instruments. Only three tiny viewports, a few inches long, showed the outside world. The pilot claimed the center port while the two scientists viewed from his right and left.

Jack Donnelly, the pilot, reported to the mother ship. "*Lulu*," he radioed. "My hatch is closed. . . . My tracking pinger and underwater phone are on, no joy [echo] on the bottom sounder. Request permission to dive."

"Roger, *Alvin*," the surface controller replied. "You are clear to dive. Present water depth is 8,700 feet. Good luck."[3]

Scuba divers stayed in the water with them for fifty feet, and then waved good-bye. At twelve hundred feet, total darkness enveloped them. The sub's lights were switched off to conserve power. "The tense feeling I had at the start of the dive is replaced by a sense of relaxation and serenity," Ballard wrote.[4] All became quiet. It took more than two hours to reach the bottom.

*Diving inside the research submersible* Alvin, *scientists could view the depths of the ocean with their own eyes.*

At eight thousand feet deep, seven hundred feet from the seafloor, the diving team came to life. They activated *Alvin*'s lights, cameras, data logger, and sonar. Through their viewports, the scientists saw swirling white flakes falling from the surface reflecting the sub's spotlight. This "marine snow" is made of decayed sea animals and plants. Two hundred feet from the bottom, Donnelly released a pair of heavy weights. The loss of five hundred pounds slowed *Alvin*'s descent abruptly. Six ballast tanks opened and filled with seawater. This caused the sub to achieve neutral buoyancy, neither rising nor sinking. It hung suspended, motionless above the seafloor.

Donnelly steered to the bottom along a sloping lava flow. *Alvin* hung from it like a mountain climber because it was too steep to land on. Five hours of observation and collecting began. *Alvin* hopped from station to station, picking up lava in its mechanical claw. Ballard and Moore concentrated as they worked the manipulator arm. Fragile or slippery samples sometimes escaped. The two scientists dictated observations nonstop into their tape recorders.

When another scientist returned from a different Project FAMOUS dive with Ballard, he found that he could not hear his own voice on his tape. Ballard's booming observations had drowned it out. The scientist fought back by taking the cardboard tube from a roll of toilet paper. He wrote "BALLARD FILTER" on it. On future dives, he spoke through it directly into the microphone.[5]

The divers broke only once, for lunch, as the tangy

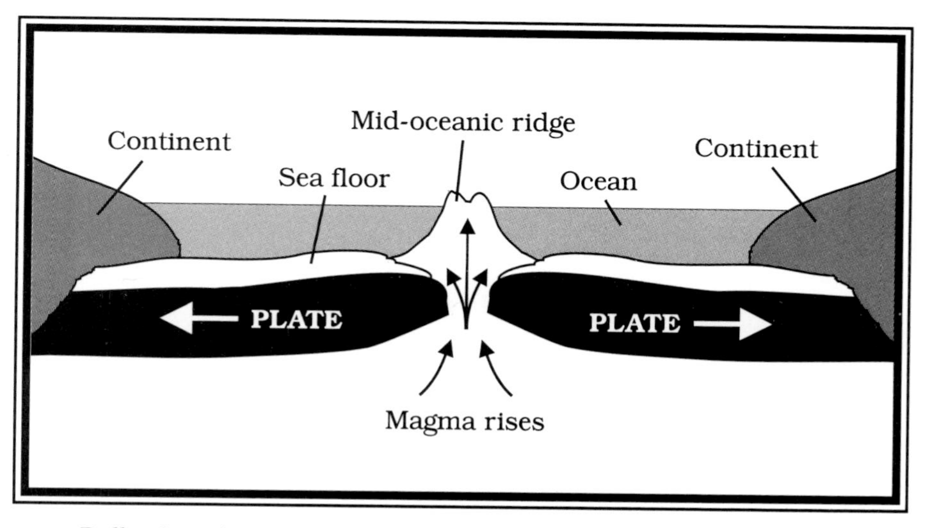


*Ballard and a team of scientists studied the ocean floor for evidence supporting the theory of continental drift, or plate tectonics. They wanted to show that lava squeezes up from the earth's interior and moves the continents.*

aroma of pepper steak sandwiches surrounded them. At mission's end they began to tire.

"*Lulu*, this is *Alvin*," Donnelly radioed. "We are running low on battery power. How does it look up there?"

The surface controller answered, "All clear. Come on up."[6]

By dropping five hundred more pounds, *Alvin* rose.

The press hailed Project FAMOUS as a great success. *Alvin* completed eighteen dives. The French undertook twenty-seven. Scientists collected three thousand pounds of rock and water samples and took more than one hundred thousand photographs.

The study confirmed that the African plate was pulling back at the rate of one inch per year. Slow as that seems, it formed the Atlantic Ocean in 260 million years. This is only a fraction of Earth's age. The scientists demonstrated that new seafloor is constantly being created from the lava that squeezes up from the earth's interior.

Ballard was awed by this earth-creation process. On one dive, *Alvin* located a crack only fifteen feet across. A powerful spotlight was aimed down it and was swallowed. The crack seemed to have no bottom. Ballard felt he was looking back into the beginning of time.

He asked the pilot to pause. "I just wanted to look at it," he remembered. The pause lasted a long time.[7]

# Mysteries of the Deep

Ballard first headed his own major geological expedition in 1976, to the Cayman Trough. This underwater rift in the Caribbean is four times as deep as the Grand Canyon.

On one *Alvin* dive there, Ballard and the pilot had trouble finding a small enough rock sample. So they put a crowbar into *Alvin*'s mechanical claw. They wedged the bar into a crack in the rock face and pulled with all of the sub's weight. For almost an hour, they struggled to pry a piece off. Over and over, the crowbar sprang free, smashing *Alvin* into the cliff. At last, they loosened a football-sized sample of rock.

As they pulled back to leave, the sub's floodlights shone on the rock they had just wrestled with. "My throat went tight and the flesh on my neck tingled," Ballard remembered. When he spoke, his voice came out tinny, "Take a look at that."[1] The rock was an enormous boulder—and it was not attached to the cliff. With one wrong move, it would have squashed them flat.

The next year, Dr. Jack Corliss, who had joined the Cayman study, invited Ballard to come on an expedition. Their destination was the Galápagos Rift, off the Pacific coast of South America. There they would search for underwater hot springs, or hydrothermal vents.

Because of Ballard's experience in deep diving as well as in conducting complicated expeditions, he was asked to be co–chief scientist of the expedition. He was also asked to supervise the use of the ANGUS system, which would be used to find the hydrothermal vents. ANGUS was an early underwater camera sled that took only still photographs. A surface ship towed it with a cable thousands of feet long. Ballard added a special thermometer to ANGUS's instrument rack. Any change in the deep ocean's frigid temperature might indicate hot springs.

The stars were brilliant the first night of work, but the tropical weather was steamy. The ANGUS crew was grateful for the cool lab on board. They had barely begun work when a graduate student tapped her pencil on the double lines of ink on a long paper scroll. "Looks like a temperature [abnormality]," she said.[2] Ballard hurried to her side. He checked to make sure it was not a computer error. For three minutes, the ink lines spread apart, then rejoined. No, it had lasted too

*This mini-ANGUS is a smaller version of the underwater camera sled ANGUS, which takes only still photographs. During an expedition, the camera sled will be attached by a strong cable, lowered into the ocean, and towed behind the research ship.*

long. He logged the exact location of the change. Had they found a hot spring on their very first try?

ANGUS had been clicking away during the temperature spike. But its run had to be completed, its cable hauled, and its film developed before the photographic evidence could be examined. The next morning, Ballard raced to the darkroom, eager to see the photos. The room was packed with scientists. They focused on the twenty shots taken at the time of the spike. What they saw astonished them.

"Clams!" Corliss exclaimed.

"Hundreds of clams," Ballard added, counting rapidly. "And look at the color of the water."[3] It was milky white.

A mile and a half from the life-giving sun, clams grew wildly. In pitch dark, on bare lava, in near-freezing water, with little to eat. And with water pressure equal to the weight of an automobile pressing down on each square inch of their bodies.

"What's going on down there?" Corliss asked.[4]

The next day, *Alvin*'s pilot followed Ballard's directions to what the scientists hoped would be a vent. For fifteen minutes, he steered across empty lava. *Alvin*'s thermometer was programmed to sound at an increase of even a hundredth of a degree. Suddenly, it beeped. The digital readout flashed red.

Corliss, aboard *Alvin*, radioed a graduate student. "Isn't the deep ocean supposed to be like a desert?" he asked. Ballard listened intently nearby.

"Yes," she answered.

"Well," Corliss said, "there's all these animals down here."[5]

Corliss's voice nearly trembled.[6]

The clams measured up to a foot across. They lay on the lava next to enormous brown mussels. Ghostly white crabs crawled over rocks heaped with spaghetti-like worms. Orange puffballs, like dandelions gone to seed, sat beside anemones and starfish. Pink-eyed fish swam lazily beside them. The water temperature registered 61 degrees Fahrenheit. Just yards away it stayed at 34 degrees.

"We are sampling a hydrothermal vent," Corliss announced.[7] He was confident that the expedition had met its goal.

"We didn't know what we were looking for," Ballard remembered. "We had an abstract idea that there would be a crack and warm water coming out of it, like a spring. But then to walk into Disneyland!"[8]

Expedition members were at dinner when water samples were opened in the chemistry lab. Suddenly, the dining room filled with the stink of rotten eggs. The ship's excellent air-conditioning system sped the smell throughout the vessel. Ballard ran to the lab but could not take the stench. Even the chief chemist had trouble breathing.

The springs gushed hot water mixed with hydrogen sulfide, a smelly and deadly poison. Yet the vent animals survived in this toxic environment. The smell provided the first clue to the mystery of how the vent community fed itself.

Almost all living creatures eat food grown using the energy of the sun. This process is called photosynthesis. Scientists, however, knew that some forms of bacteria living in swamps used chemicals called sulfides as food. These swamps, too, smelled like rotten eggs. This rare process was called chemosynthesis. It depended on chemical reactions, not the sun, for energy.

Hydrothermal vent animals were too far from the sun to find food produced by photosynthesis. Instead, like swamp bacteria, they used chemosynthesis. At the bottom of the vent's unique food chain were bacteria living inside the porous lava. They fed on sulfides from the water. Other microbes ate them and were eaten, in turn, by larger and larger creatures. The energy to set this chain in motion came not from the sun but from the heat of the earth's interior.

"We realized we had stumbled onto a major scientific discovery," Ballard said. "I saw normally [serious scientists] skipping with pleasure."[9]

When Ballard took his turn in *Alvin*, he was thrilled. "After many years, deep diving had become routine for me—but not that day," he said.[10]

Above the vents, he saw the milky water appear to shimmer. "Let's get a sample of that flaky stuff," Ballard suggested.[11] The water was so full of minerals and bacteria, it caused an optical illusion. The most amazing animals of all were the giant red worms in hard white tubes. They grew so thick at one spot that scientists named it the "Garden of Eden."

What was the meaning of all this? Ballard and the other scientists spent many late tropical nights tossing around ideas. Corliss immediately began to wonder whether life on Earth could have begun in hydrothermal vents. Thermal springs have existed for

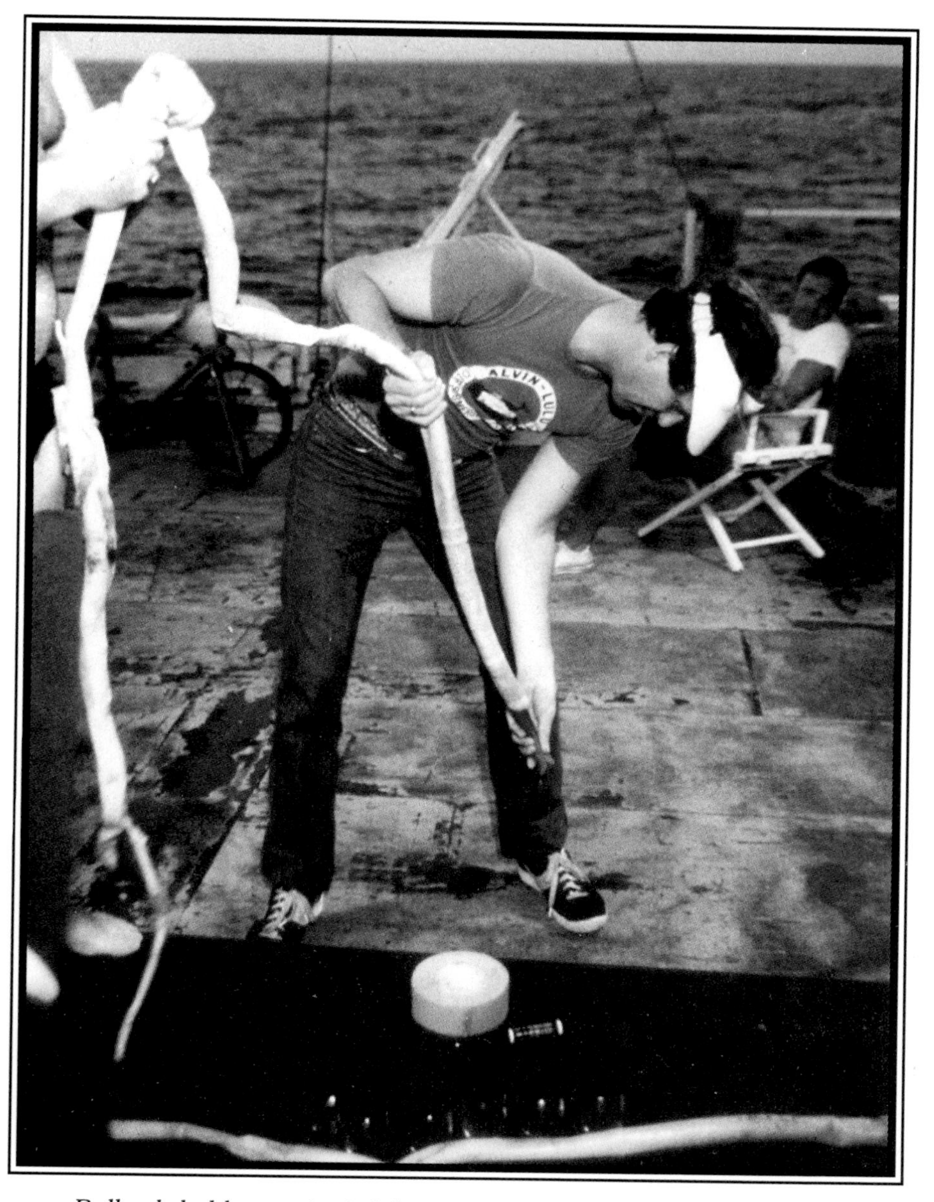


*Ballard holds a giant tube worm from the Galápagos Rift thermal vent. These amazing creatures live more than a mile below the ocean's surface.*

2 to 3.5 billion years, long before living creatures. "We now know that these sites are friendly to life," Ballard wrote. "[They] could have provided an excellent environment for life's first development from lifeless molecules."[12]

Earth may not be the only planet with hydrothermal vents. The surface of at least one of Jupiter's moons is frozen. But scientists suspect that seafloor lava tubes may hide beneath it. We know that life can exist on Earth under similar conditions. Does that mean there could be giant tube worms in space? Ballard, for one, believes it is possible.[13]

Many years later, Ballard was being interviewed in an online chat on the Internet. One questioner asked him to name his greatest discovery. To everyone's surprise, he answered, "Well, it wasn't the *Titanic*. . . . My greatest discovery was . . . of exotic creatures living around underwater hot springs."[14]

One night during the expedition, Ballard and a fellow scientist relaxed on the ship's deck with a cold drink. Far below, ANGUS was at work. They discussed their feelings about the expedition's amazing accomplishments. "You know, Bob," the other scientist said. "This is what it must have been like sailing with Columbus."[15] Ballard agreed.

# The Door Swings Open

In 1977, Robert Ballard met the man who shared his dream of finding the *Titanic*. Bill Tantum, "Mr. Titanic," was the president of the *Titanic* Historical Society. He lent Ballard books from his collection. He told him story after fascinating story. "As I listened to Bill," Ballard remembered, "I began to understand the full dimensions of the tragedy and to acquire some of his passion for the ship."[1] Tantum urged him to plan an expedition.

In 1978 and 1979, Ballard made several more cruises to hydrothermal vent sites. *Alvin* had been modified since Ballard's last voyage. A video camera had been mounted on *Alvin*'s exterior, and a color monitor inside the sub displayed the picture. A strange thing happened as a result.

Ballard watched, fascinated, as his fellow scientists turned away from *Alvin*'s tiny viewports. They looked at the video screen instead. "Wait a minute," he thought. "We went through a tremendous amount of trouble to bring these people halfway around the earth, get them all the way down here in a submarine—and they turn their backs to the windows!" A seed was planted in Ballard's fertile brain. "Clearly, they thought they could do a better job looking through a robot's eyes, rather than through their own."[2]

Ballard's next destination was off the Mexican Pacific Coast, near Baja California. More amazing discoveries awaited scientists there. Earlier dives had revealed the presence of hollow tubes of sulfide at the bottom of the sea. Instruments showed temperature abnormalities. Could this be a different type of hydrothermal vent?

Ballard eagerly awaited his turn to dive. "My first view of the billowing smokestack[s] sent a shiver of amazement down my back," he wrote. His dive partner said, "They seem connected to hell itself." It was precisely what Ballard had been thinking.[3] The scientists carried a new temperature probe. This time they took an exact reading: 662 degrees Fahrenheit—hot enough to melt lead.

The "black smokers," as they came to be called, were formed when superheated water flowing up from around the magma chamber came into contact with cold seawater. Sulfide-rich minerals poured out so thickly that the dark mineral cloud looked like smoke. Gradually the chimneys hardened and grew taller, as high as thirty feet. The discoveries of this expedition would be studied for years to come.

Ballard moved his family to Palo Alto, California, in 1980. He took a year's sabbatical from work, a time to study, write, and plan. There, at Stanford University in Silicon Valley, he encountered the new computer and fiber optics industries. This was the technology he had been waiting for.

For years, Ballard had been frustrated by the limitations of submersibles. It takes five hours just to sink to the level of the deep ocean and then come back up, he told an interviewer. You only get three hours of productive work while you are there, because of the limits of battery power. "Think of how much more ground you could cover if you didn't have to worry about human passengers and could just let a robot act as your eyes under the sea."[4]

Ballard began to envision a new super-ANGUS robot. Like ANGUS, it would be a towed camera sled. But this robot would not just shoot black-and-white still photos that would be developed and viewed hours after they were taken. It would use multiple color-video cameras. These would be connected to the mother ship by fiber-optic cable. The video images could then be viewed by scientists aboard ship in "real time," as they were being shot.

And what if a second, smaller, nimbler robot could be attached to the first? What if it was motorized, not towed, and could navigate under its own power? What a tool for exploration it would be! Ballard was energized by this vision. He already knew what to call his robots. The little explorer would be *Jason*, named for

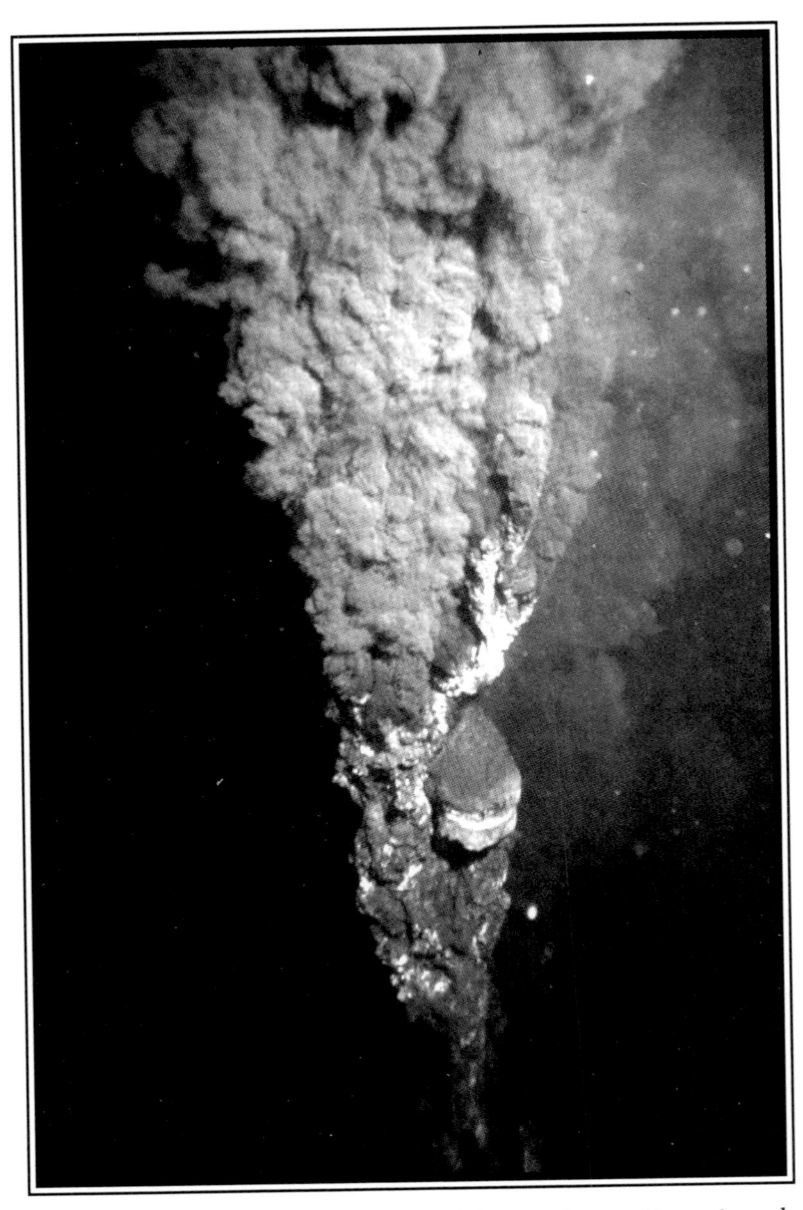

*This "black smoker" at the bottom of the sea is spouting mineral-rich water hot enough to melt lead. Robert Ballard was a member of the expedition that discovered smokers in 1979.*

the ancient Greek mythical hero. The sled would be *Argo*, just like Jason's ship.

While Ballard was in California, he was shaken by unexpected news. A *Titanic* search was being mounted. Two well-known geologists would lead the search. Jack Grimm, a flamboyant Texas oil millionaire, had bankrolled them. Grimm had previously made headlines financing unsuccessful searches for Noah's Ark, the Loch Ness Monster, and the Abominable Snowman.

Then a second blow fell. Bill Tantum died suddenly of a stroke in June 1980. Ballard mourned the loss of his friend and staunchest supporter.[5]

The Grimm expedition began in July. Before sailing, Grimm arranged for a monkey named Titan to join the cruise. Titan was to point to a map of the North Atlantic. Grimm predicted the *Titanic* would be found where the monkey's finger indicated. The embarrassed scientists demanded the monkey's removal. "Fire the scientists," Grimm replied.[6] Luckily, someone talked him out of it.

The expedition failed. Bad weather and equipment failures plagued the searchers. A follow-up cruise in 1981 was equally unsuccessful. Meanwhile, Ballard returned to his research at Woods Hole. Slowly, he began to put together a multimillion-dollar funding package to develop the *Argo–Jason* system. His chief benefactor was the U.S. Navy (both the Office of Naval Research and the Director of Submarine Warfare). The Navy was particularly interested in *Argo–Jason*'s potential for deep-ocean searches and knew just what it wanted Ballard to look for. Two nuclear submarines, *Thresher* and *Scorpion*, had been lost in the

1960s. The Navy needed detailed information about the wrecks.

With Navy backing, Ballard founded the Deep Submergence Laboratory at Woods Hole in 1982. Its purpose was to develop underwater robots, most specifically *Argo* and *Jason*. Ballard built a team of high-tech engineers. These computer scientists and robotics specialists had the expertise to make his vision a reality. Jack Grimm made a final attempt to locate the *Titanic* in 1983. Once again he failed. Ballard was still in the race.

In early 1984, an experimental *Argo* was nearly ready. The Navy agreed to fund a two-step field test of the robot. In the summer of 1984, Ballard and his Woods Hole team would explore the *Thresher* wreck site with *Argo*. Then, in the summer of 1985, they would have three weeks to do the same for *Scorpion*. Three weeks, Ballard thought, that was more than enough time. With the remaining time, perhaps they could do some additional field testing. Maybe they could look for the *Titanic*.

Ballard ran into the *Argo* workshop as soon as he got the good news. "Gentlemen," he told his team, "our time has come. The door to the *Titanic*'s tomb has just swung open."[7]

Ballard promptly flew to Paris to arrange a partnership with the French government. He had maintained close ties to French oceanographers since the days of Project FAMOUS. Unlike the United States, France generously funded oceanographic research. A governmental agency, IFREMER, considered Ballard's proposal. The French agreed to combine resources. Ballard's friend Jean-Louis Michel would be the expedition's coleader.

In July 1984, Ballard and his team field-tested the experimental *Argo*. They sailed 240 miles east of Cape Cod, to the spot where the Navy's nuclear sub *Thresher* went down in 1963. One hundred twenty-nine sailors and civilian workers had died when the sub lost power and sank below "crush depth." The enormous pressure caused by the weight of the ocean had crushed the nearly three-hundred-foot vessel.

After two days at the wreck site, Ballard was perplexed. He knew from other divers' accounts that most sites looked the same. The main wreck lies inside its impact crater. Around it lies a circle of debris.

The *Thresher* site looked different. *Argo* had spent two days "mowing the lawn" around the main wreck. The Navy wanted the site meticulously mapped. Yet there appeared to be very little debris on one side of the wreck. On the other side, it seemed to trail off endlessly. Ballard sat thinking in the *Argo* control room. Classical music played softly on the stereo. Instrument panels hummed, blinked, and clicked. He stared at a video monitor as *Thresher* debris flew by. Suddenly, he understood.

"It's not a circle," he whispered to himself. "It's got to be a trail."[8]

When a vessel falls into very deep water, he realized, it makes a pattern different from that of a shallow-water wreck. The heaviest debris, including the vessel itself, falls straight down. Lighter debris is

caught by the current. In a long, slow fall, it spreads out in a trail, following the direction of the current.

*Thresher* lay in 8,500 feet of water. The *Titanic* was at almost thirteen thousand feet. Years before, Ballard and Tantum had decided on a *Titanic* search area of one hundred square miles. Looking for the ship in this large a plot was like searching for a needle in a haystack. But what if Ballard were to search for the *Titanic*'s debris trail instead? That would cover a much larger area.

For the next year, leading up to their summer 1985 cruise, Ballard and his team had tasks to complete. At Woods Hole, they would race to complete the perfected *Argo*. Ballard and Michel would restudy the historic record. They would pore over survivors' accounts, ships' logbooks, weather and current records. They would decide on the best possible search strategy. They knew the key to their success lay in the events of that fateful night.

# A Night to Remember

It was 11:35 P.M., Sunday, April 14, 1912. First Officer Murdoch scanned the horizon for icebergs. High above in the crow's nest, two lookouts did the same. All three men knew the *Titanic* had received some ice warnings by telegraph from other ships. Yet none of them realized that the great liner was steaming directly into a seventy-eight-mile-long ice field. The seven separate messages had never been connected.

Murdoch stood on the *Titanic*'s bridge, on its highest deck. Next to him, Quartermaster Robert Hichens took the ship's wheel. Captain Edward Smith had gone to bed. The night was bitterly cold and very dark, yet perfectly calm.

Still, the men watched carefully. Suddenly, Lookout Frederick Fleet saw a vague but monstrous shape loom up from the blackness. He struck the warning bell three times, then telephoned the bridge. "Iceberg right ahead," he cried.[1] Murdoch ordered Hichens to turn the wheel as sharply as possible. Thirty-seven seconds passed. It seemed like an eternity to the anxious Fleet before the enormous liner turned to the left.[2] The *Titanic* ground slightly against the berg. Several tons of ice toppled into the forward well deck. Some passengers playfully kicked ball-sized chunks to one another.

Almost nine hundred feet back, the officer on duty at the stern doubted his senses. He thought he saw an old-fashioned windjammer under full sail glide by. Then he realized it was a hundred-foot-high iceberg. He watched it disappear behind the ship into the darkness.

The iceberg had sliced open twelve square feet of the *Titanic*'s hull. Seawater poured in. Few of the more than two thousand people aboard even realized something had happened. Yet the *Titanic* was doomed.

In second-class cabin number eight, six decks below the bridge, Mrs. A. O. Becker had just fallen asleep. Her three children, twelve-year-old Ruth, four-year-old Marion, and one-year-old Richard, slept nearby. Her husband, a missionary in India, was not on board the ship with the family. Abruptly, Mrs. Becker awoke. Something felt wrong. The ship was quiet and still. There was no vibration from the ship's massive engines. The *Titanic* had stopped in the middle of the ocean.

The worried Mrs. Becker asked a passing steward what was wrong.[3] "There's nothing wrong at all," he replied. "There's just a little accident and they're going to fix it."[4]

By now Captain Smith had gotten up. He and his officers viewed the damage. Only twenty minutes after impact, twenty-four feet of water filled the bow. Letters floated in the mail room. Five minutes later, the squash court was submerged. Thomas Andrews, the *Titanic*'s builder, was aboard for the maiden voyage. He grimly assessed the situation for Smith. The ship would sink in one to one and a half hours, Andrews predicted. The captain ordered the wireless operators to send out a call for help to nearby ships. Then he gave the command to ready the lifeboats.

By this time, young Ruth Becker was awake. "There was so much noise upstairs," she said. "[They were] running in the halls and yelling."[5] She and her mother waited fifteen minutes, then hailed another passing steward. This time they were told, "Put on your things and come at once."

"Do we have time to dress?" Mrs. Becker asked.

"No, madam," he answered. "You have time for nothing."[6]

At 12:25 A.M., Monday, April 15, the order was given to abandon ship and load the lifeboats. There were only twenty lifeboats and more than twenty-two hundred passengers. The captain was well aware how few of them would survive.

Women and children first was the time-honored

rule of the sea. Some crew members were assigned to row each boat. The Beckers hurried to a large room filled with women "in all kinds of dress or undress," Ruth remembered. "They were crying or they were scared because they didn't know what was going to happen."[7] Ruth wore a coat over her nightgown. She had put on shoes and socks but not a life jacket.

Twenty minutes later, the first lifeboat was lowered. Like many of the early boats, it was still half-empty. Passengers refused to leave the *Titanic*. Some could not believe they would be safer in a rowboat on the open sea than on the stately liner. The lights still blazed. The ship's band played cheerful tunes to keep everyone's spirits up. Some women refused to leave their husbands. The elderly Ida Straus told her husband, Macy's founder Isidor Straus, "Where you go, I go."[8] The crew did not reveal the full extent of the danger, for they did not wish to cause a panic. Some even told the lifeboats' passengers they would be back for breakfast.

In their office, the telegraph operators feverishly tapped out the distress call in Morse code. One of them, Harold Bride, had an idea. He suggested that they try the brand-new signal for help: S-O-S, S-O-S traveled across the airwaves for the first time anywhere. Numerous ships heard the call but were too far away. The *Carpathia* was only fifty-eight miles distant. Her captain, Arthur Rostron, immediately headed to the *Titanic*'s rescue. He informed the telegraphers that his ship was "coming along as fast as we can."[9]

On the *Titanic*, a distress rocket was launched as

*This photograph of one of the* Titanic's *lifeboats was taken from a rescuing ship.*

a beacon for approaching ships. A gasp went up from the waiting passengers. Lawrence Beesley, a teacher, remembered them all saying at once, "Rockets!" He added, "Anybody knows what rockets at sea mean."[10] Many passengers realized for the first time that the ship was sinking.

The bow began to pitch down noticeably as it filled with water. Passengers in lifeboats floating nearby could see the low waves lap against the *Titanic*'s name on the hull. The telegraph operators signaled desperately, "We are sinking fast. . . . Women and children in boats. Cannot last much longer."[11]

The Beckers huddled with other women and

children, awaiting instructions. Finally, they were told to climb an iron ladder to the boat deck. Lifeboat No. 11 was filling as they arrived. One officer snatched little Marion Becker, and another took baby Richard. They plopped the children into the boat and shouted, "That's all for this boat."

Mrs. Becker shrieked, "Please let me in that boat. Those are my children!"[12]

She jumped in as the boat descended, leaving her oldest daughter behind. "Ruth," she screamed, "get in another boat."[13]

It was now 1:30 A.M. The hour and a half Thomas Andrews had predicted for the ship to remain afloat was over. The *Titanic* was living on borrowed time.

Ruth moved to the next lifeboat, No. 13. A crying woman stood there pleading, "Don't put me in the boat . . . I've never been in an open boat in my life."[14] Ruth politely asked an officer's permission to board. He lifted her up and dropped her in as the boat filled to capacity. The order was given to lower. Officers on deck used ropes and pulleys to let down first the front of the boat, then the rear, then the front, then the rear. The passengers felt each jerk as they sloped up and down repeatedly on their way to the sea some sixty feet below. "But I was never scared," said Ruth later. "I was only excited. I never for one minute thought we would die."[15] She could see hundreds of faces gazing down at her as she suddenly realized only one lifeboat remained on that side.

On the other side of the ship, several lifeboats were loading. John Jacob Astor, one of the world's richest men, helped his pregnant young wife aboard

No. 4. He asked permission to join her and was refused. He demanded to know the lifeboat's number and turned away.

When Ruth's lifeboat, No. 13, hit the surface, it was pushed backward by a rush of exhaust water from the ship's pumps. The lowering ropes were still attached. They immediately became so tight they could not be released. Directly overhead was No. 15, coming down fast. The people in No. 13 were going to be crushed. The screaming passengers could actually stand and touch No. 15's hull in a hopeless attempt to push it away. At the last minute, two sailors drew their knives and sliced through No. 13's straining ropes. The boat slid clear just in time.

The oarsmen rowed away as fast as possible. They stopped about a mile away. "It was [a] very, very dark, black night," Ruth remembered, "and the ocean was very calm. Just like a millpond." Though there was no moon, the stars were brilliant. From a distance "the [*Titanic*] was just beautiful," she said.[16] It looked like a "great, lighted theater," one of the oarsmen agreed.[17]

The huge ship was now so far down at the bow that the propellers stood out of the water. Yet all the portholes, even those under the sea, shone brightly. Snatches of music drifted through the night. The *Titanic*'s valiant band was still playing. "There were five or six decks and they were just lined with people standing at the edge looking over," remembered Ruth. "I suppose they were wishing and hoping someone would come and rescue them."[18] The time was 2:05 A.M., and all the lifeboats were gone. Incredibly, no law had required the *Titanic* to provide lifeboat space for all aboard.

The air temperature was below freezing, and the water was ice-cold. Some of the crewmen rowing No. 13 were engine-room workers, shivering in shirts and shorts. Ruth gave them the blankets she carried. She bandaged one stoker's injured hand with her father's handkerchief. Next to her, a young woman sobbed uncontrollably. Another passenger translated the woman's German cries. Her infant had gone off alone in No. 11, in the same boat as Ruth's family.

At 2:10 A.M. on the ship, Captain Smith released the telegraph operators. "Men, you have done your full duty," he told them. "You can do no more. Abandon your cabin. Now it's every man for himself."[19]

As the bow sank lower, the stern climbed higher. The fifteen hundred passengers still aboard moved up and to the rear in a great mass. They looked, from a distance, like a swarm of bees clinging to the ship. At 2:18 A.M. a tremendous roar was heard. The ship's stern pointed almost straight up. Everything movable aboard the ship came crashing down. Ruth Becker heard screams and saw people jump overboard. Then the great ship broke in two. The bow plunged into the sea. The stern settled back horizontally for an instant. Then it tilted, twirled around, and gently slid under. A single voice on lifeboat No. 13 spoke: "She's gone; that's the last of her."[20] It was 2:20 A.M.

But the horror was not over. "There fell upon the ear the most terrible noise that human beings ever listened to," said Ruth, "the cries of hundreds of people struggling in the icy cold water, crying for help with a cry we knew could not be answered."[21] Almost eighty years later she would say, "I can still hear them."[22]

For an hour, the oarsmen rowed aimlessly just to keep warm. The other survivors had never felt such piercing cold. In No. 13, a steward found six handkerchiefs in his pockets and gave them to the hatless. They tied the corners together to fashion little caps. One of the thinly dressed stokers fell listlessly to the bottom of the boat. Suddenly, someone saw a glow in the southeast. The stoker lay still. Then a faint boom was heard. The stoker sat bolt upright. "That was a cannon," he cried.[23]

It was the *Carpathia*, firing rockets as she sped to the rescue. She came aside the first lifeboat at 4:10 A.M. Dawn was breaking. All around them, the survivors could see hundreds of icebergs glowing pink in the sunrise. "Look at the beautiful North Pole with no Santa Claus on it," said little Douglas Spedden in boat No. 3.[24] On the *Carpathia*, an amazed Captain Rostron looked around at the ice field he had just steamed through in the dark. "I shuddered," the deeply religious captain said, "and could only think that some other Hand than mine was on the helm during the night."[25]

Ruth's lifeboat was tied to the side of the *Carpathia* at 4:45 A.M. Some survivors climbed up a ladder to the rescue ship. Others were hoisted up by ropes. When Ruth's turn came, she was so numb with cold that her hands would not grasp the lines. She was tied into a swing and hauled up. *Carpathia*'s officers and doctors met each survivor with blankets and hot drinks. Ruth was offered coffee and brandy. Being only twelve, she had never tasted alcohol. But she could not drink anything. "I was so worried about my mother," she said.[26] The last lifeboat was emptied at 8:30 A.M.

Ruth helped the frantic German mother search for her missing infant. All around them distraught women looked hopelessly for their husbands. Ruth had seen no sign of her own family. They searched for two hours. Finally, a woman approached them. "Is your name Ruth Becker?" she asked. Ruth answered yes. "Well, your mother has been looking everywhere for you," the woman said. "So I was reunited with my mother and my brother and my sister and they were all right," Ruth remembered.[27] And at last, the German woman had a joyful reunion with her baby.

Captain Rostron held a religious service for the 705 survivors. They gave thanks for their lives and offered prayers for the dead. At 12:30 P.M. the ship steamed in a circle before turning toward New York. All that could be seen on the water was one floating deck chair. It was the survivors' last glimpse of any trace of the *Titanic*. None of them would see the great ship again for seventy-three years.

# Titanic Hero

The coordinates of the R.M.S. *Titanic* as she sent out her distress call were 41°46' N, 50°14' W. These were perhaps the most famous lines of latitude and longitude in the history of seafaring. In this patch of the North Atlantic, the International Ice Patrol dropped a wreath every April 15. Surely it would be easy to find the *Titanic*'s grave. Yet Jack Grimm's three expeditions had not been able to do so. Why not?

Robert Ballard asked himself this question. He knew that the coordinates were based on celestial navigation. This was an ancient but sometimes unreliable method of gauging latitude and longitude by the sun and stars. It was clear now that the *Titanic*'s navigator had erred in estimating her location based on

the last fix hours before the collision, at sunset. But by how much and in what direction?

Ballard and Jean-Louis Michel had two other sets of coordinates to work with. They knew the liner should be on the eastern side of the massive ice field that stopped or slowed so many ships that night. They knew where the lifeboats had been picked up. A strong current had pushed them steadily south to their rescue. So they laid out a rectangle of 150 square miles. They predicted that the *Titanic* would lie within it.

Ballard expected the French to locate the *Titanic* while the Woods Hole team surveyed the *Scorpion* site. Then a combined team would use the *Argo* video sled to photograph what remained of the most famous wreck in the world.

For six weeks, the French patiently mowed the lawn with their powerful deep-towed sonar. Nothing. There was no sign of the ship. The short period of good summer weather in the North Atlantic was ending. The French ship had to return to Europe. The Woods Hole vessel *Knorr* took her place on August 24.

Ballard and Michel altered their search strategy. The *Thresher* expedition had yielded the key to finding deepwater wrecks. The *Scorpion* search confirmed it. The team would search not for the *Titanic* but for her debris field. Like an arrow, it would point to the ship. They would start at the lifeboat recovery point and work north. They had only until September 5 to succeed. Then *Knorr* would have to return to Woods Hole for its next assignment.

They saw nothing but mud for a week on their

video monitors. It was after midnight on September 1, and *Argo* engineer Tom Dettweiler slept in his cabin. Suddenly, his door was thrown open with a terrific crash. "We got it!" someone screamed.

"Who was that?" Dettweiler's roommate asked, as they frantically threw their clothes on in the dark.

"That was Ballard," he answered. "We knew from his excitement," Dettweiler remembered, "that we had indeed found it."[1] A circular object had appeared minutes earlier on the video monitors. Examination of photographs of the *Titanic*'s massive boilers proved an exact match.

They had found the arrow. Now to follow it to its target. *Knorr*'s echo sounder quickly located the hull. But for twenty-four hours the team surveyed the debris field, cautiously skirting the main wreck. "A million questions surged through my mind," said Ballard.[2] Was the *Titanic* upright or on its side or upside down? Were the rigging and smokestacks waiting to entangle *Argo*? And most ghastly of all, would they find human remains?

On September 2, they were ready to tow *Argo* over the ship. Scientists and crew packed the control room. Everyone wanted to see the great liner. At first, the video sled flew so high it showed only a blur. Then the magnetometer operator reported, "I have a massive object off to starboard on sonar; we're about to cross it."[3]

"It was now or never," Ballard remembered. "We're going down," he directed.[4]

The crowd in the control room gasped. If the masts or smokestacks still stood, *Argo*'s cable could become entangled. The multimillion-dollar video sled would be lost, and their first view of the *Titanic* would be their last. Then the video monitor showed the faint outline of a hull.

"It's the side of the ship. She's upright," Ballard exclaimed.[5]

They began to cross the ship on the right (starboard) side. A gaping hole outlined where the forward smokestack had stood. It had toppled before the ship split in two, narrowly missing telegraph operator Harold Bride in the water. Then they passed over the bridge, where Murdoch and Hichens had stood watch at the moment of impact with the iceberg. The bridge was flattened, reduced to a mere outline. They approached the bow.

"Then I saw it," Ballard said, "the unmistakable image of a boat davit."[6] From these empty hooks, or davits, had hung one of the too-few lifeboats. "It hit me square in the stomach," he remembered.[7]

*Argo* crossed the ship two more times. They saw that the Number Two smokestack had also fallen. They viewed the opening over the Grand Staircase, its glass ceiling now shattered and gone. A tangled mass of twisted steel exposed the ship's innards. The stern was completely missing.

Outside, the weather had turned ugly. It was too dangerous to tow *Argo*, so ANGUS and its still cameras went to work. They snapped hundreds of close-up color photos of the debris field. The pictures documented the contents of the ship, which had spilled to the bottom. China teacups, silver serving platters, headboards, bedsprings, hundreds of bottles of wine. They saw no human remains, but they did find shoes. Always in pairs, always side by side. "These were terribly moving scenes," says Ballard.[8] The photographs also revealed the shattered wreck of the stern. It lay about two thousand feet south of the bow.

With twenty-four hours remaining, ANGUS made a final close-up sweep of the hull from front to back. The stunning color photos showed anchor chains still in place. They were next to polished brass fixtures, looking brand-new. Cargo cranes were slammed to the deck. So was the mast with the crow's nest still attached. From his post there, Lookout Fleet had sighted the killer iceberg. At 5:56 A.M. on September 5, 1985, Ballard heard the captain call, "You have to start up now."[9] Ballard had been working around the clock for four and a half days.

Giddy from lack of sleep, he headed to the radio room to conduct interviews. While the Woods Hole team labored, the news media had gone wild. The *Titanic* had been found! Patiently, Ballard answered question after question. Then, as he talked to NBC-TV newscaster Tom Brokaw, he glanced out a nearby porthole. The ship was under way. They were going home.

"We were leaving and I hadn't said good-bye," Ballard remembered. "I got choked up and couldn't talk. I had to get back to the fantail and make my peace."[10] He hung up on Brokaw.

Ballard and his team returned to a hero's welcome at Woods Hole. Flags and balloons flew. A band played, a cannon boomed, and reporters filled the docks. Ballard insisted on a private reunion with his wife and sons first. "Having my family there was really important to me. They had paid a big price over the years during my long months away from home, but they'd never once complained," he said.[11]

Then he made an eloquent statement to the world:

> *The* Titanic *lies in 13,000 feet of water on a gently sloping alpine-like countryside overlooking a small canyon below. Its bow faces north and the ship sits upright on the bottom. There is no light at this great depth and little life can be found. It is a quiet and peaceful and fitting place for the remains of this greatest of sea tragedies to rest. May it forever remain this way. . . .*[12]

To help ensure that the *Titanic* remain undisturbed, Ballard refused to reveal its exact location.

Ballard's life would never be the same. Now he was a famous man. "You've done a lot of good science," his mother said. "Hope you survive the *Titanic*."[13] "She's afraid now," Ballard explained, "that that's all anyone is going to know about me."[14]

Fulfilling his dream had other unexpected consequences. "I didn't expect the *Titanic* to hit me emotionally. . . . A disaster put to rest seventy-three, seventy-four years ago came roaring back into the present like a freight train," he said.[15] Each teacup, each boot, each lifeboat davit reminded him of a life lost. He had come to know the *Titanic*'s passengers through his research. It was like seeing them all die once again.

Ballard went into seclusion with his family for several months. On a December 1985 scientific cruise to the hydrothermal vents near Baja California, he formed new goals. He planned to perfect the robotic deep-submergence technology he had first envisioned in 1980. It was time to develop *Jason*. He would return with a small, remote-controlled robot to the *Titanic* the following year. The new robot would actually explore inside the wreck.

The Deep Submergence Laboratory team at Woods Hole went into high gear. They took an old Navy ROV (remotely operated vehicle) and used it as the basis for a new robot. They named it *Jason Junior*. It would be the prototype for a full-powered *Jason*. *JJ*, as it was nicknamed, consisted of a video camera inside a motorized blue box. A bright yellow, 250-foot wire would connect it to *Alvin*, not *Argo*, not yet. An operator inside *Alvin* would use a joystick to make this "swimming eyeball" dart and hover like a hummingbird.[16]

The second *Titanic* expedition sailed from Woods Hole on July 9, 1986. This time they headed straight to the coordinates where the wreck of the *Titanic* lay. Ballard had successfully kept the location secret for a full year.

Ballard's first *Alvin* dive, on July 13, almost ended in failure. The tracking system, allowing the *Atlantis II* to locate *Alvin* at the bottom of the sea, malfunctioned. The surface controller knew where the *Titanic* lay, but not where *Alvin* was in relation to it. *Alvin*'s own sonar broke. Ballard knew only what was visible directly through the sub's viewports, not what surrounded him. A leak in the sub's battery set off a piercing alarm.

Somewhere not far away from the sub, nearly

thirteen thousand feet under the waters of the Atlantic, the *Titanic*'s hull was mired in bottom mud. It was as tall as an eleven-story building, but *Alvin* could not find it. Ballard and the two pilots made an educated guess about the location. They drove along the seafloor on *Alvin*'s single ski-like runner.

Ballard was mightily frustrated. "I'd waited thirteen long years for this moment," he fretted, "and now, a stone's throw away from my dream, I was trapped inside a sardine can on my hands and knees staring at nothing but mud."[17]

Suddenly, the tracking began working again. "*Titanic* should bear fifty yards to the west of your present location," the surface controller told them.[18] Ballard peered intently through the viewport. Then he saw a change in the bottom terrain. The rolling mud angled up steeply. It looked as if it had been pushed there by a giant bulldozer. And then it appeared. A slab of steel towered over them, rippling with rust. The rivets in the hull plates were clearly visible. Unquestionably, they saw the *Titanic* with their own eyes. "I let out my breath," Ballard remembered. "I didn't realize I had been holding it."[19]

The glimpse was brief. *Alvin* dropped its descent weights and began to rise. The battery leak had reached the critical point. *Alvin* could no longer risk losing its power. Crews worked all night replacing the battery. The next day's dive would test the strength of the *Titanic*'s deck after decades in salt water. Could *Alvin* land safely on the ship? Could a landing be made near enough to the Grand Staircase for *JJ* to explore the ship's interior?

*The remote-controlled robot* Jason Junior *was like a "swimming eyeball" sent ahead to explore. Suddenly, out of the darkness, Ballard saw the* Titanic's *knifelike bow.*

Ballard descended again the next day. His second view of the *Titanic* was "breathtaking," Ballard said. "Out of the darkness loomed the razor's edge of the bow," seeming about to mow *Alvin* down.[20] Of course, it was an illusion. The bow was buried in sixty feet of mud.

*Alvin* rose from the seafloor beside the hull. "The whole ship is bleeding rust," Ballard marveled.[21] Icicles of frothy rust dangled in the current. They disintegrated at *Alvin*'s touch. Ballard dubbed them "rusticles" and the name stuck. *Alvin*'s lights reflected off the intact glass of numerous portholes. They reminded Ballard of cat's eyes, gleaming in the dark. He counted the portholes to estimate where the *Titanic*'s name should appear on the hull. There seemed to be no trace of it. Later, videotapes would suggest the ghostly outline of the letter C.

*Alvin* made two test landings. The first was on the forward deck, next to the fallen mast. The pilot delicately lowered the sub. They heard a slight creaking. It was possible it would be the last noise they would hear before crashing into the ship's interior, never to escape. With a "muffled, crunching noise" they landed.[22] The deck held.

The bridge served as their second landing pad. Another eerie sight greeted them there. A bronze pedestal, which had supported the ship's wheel, stood alone on the deck. Wood-eating mollusks had consumed the wheel itself, the one Hichens had turned so sharply, but too late.

*JJ* would not descend the Grand Staircase yet, however. The robot had developed a leak and needed repair. Ballard satisfied himself with a long inspection of the staircase opening. It was almost large enough to admit *Alvin* itself. Ballard vowed to succeed at entering the wreck the next day.[23]

Ballard popped a cassette into the tape player as *Alvin* descended on July 15. The rousing theme music from the movies *E.T.* and *Raiders of the Lost Ark* would inspire his crew for the day's challenge. The sub headed for the Grand Staircase entrance promptly after reaching the bottom.

"Brave new world, Martin, you ready?" asked Ballard of *JJ* controller Martin Bowen.

"Yup," said Bowen.[24]

Gradually, *JJ* inched out of its garage. It hovered in the current briefly before disappearing into the yawning hole. All *Alvin*'s occupants could see was *JJ*'s yellow tether slowly paying out.

"*Alvin*, this is the *Atlantis II*. *Jason* is inside the staircase, over." Ballard's voice may have sounded calm, but in his excitement he had reversed the names of the two vessels.[25]

*JJ* hugged the wall of the staircase landing. A beautifully carved wooden clock had once graced it. Like most of the ship's wood, it was gone now. So was the elaborate paneling and even the steps.

Ballard and his crew could see through *JJ*'s eyes via a video monitor on *Alvin*. The water inside the staircase swirled with rust and debris. *JJ* entered the staircase's foyer. Faint outlines of pillars appeared through the murk. *JJ* turned for a closer look.

Suddenly, Bowen spoke, very softly. "Look at that chandelier."

*Amazingly, this crystal-beaded chandelier survived the wreck of the* Titanic. *A feathery creature called a sea pen is growing from its side.*

"No it can't be a chandelier," Ballard argued. "It couldn't possibly have survived."[26]

Yet it had. A crystal-beaded light fixture hung askew from its electrical wire. Would *JJ* be able to approach it safely, without damaging it? This would be another test of *JJ*'s value. The little ROV drew near, exploding several rusticles hanging from the ceiling. When the orange dust cleared, Ballard could see the designs traced in the light's brass base, even an empty bulb socket inside.

The day was a triumph. "Ballard had filled his promise . . . to penetrate a wreck," said Martin Bowen. "I had never seen him so jubilant as on the ride up from that dive."[27]

Ballard's vision of a tiny, tethered robot capable of close-up undersea exploration had become a reality. It was the first step toward "telepresence," Ballard's dream for scientists to do oceanographic research from the surface. Robots would be their eyes and hands, but oceanographers would feel and learn exactly as if they were there. It would be safer and use expedition time more profitably.

And he had another idea. Not only scientists would benefit from this new technology. He would bring its wonders to children and schools. They, too, would feel and learn as if they were on the bottom of the sea themselves.

# History Under the Sea

Ballard began making contacts in the business and educational communities to promote his idea. He decided to name the project after the ancient Greek hero Jason. This legendary explorer had inspired the naming of Ballard's ROVs as well. He hoped that schoolchildren would become authentic participants in voyages of scientific discovery as part of his JASON Project.

One of the first sponsors of the project was the National Geographic Society. Ballard had written articles for its magazine since 1975. The society's television broadcast *Secrets of the Titanic* thrilled the world with the first video images of the wreck. The society agreed to film the JASON Project's first expedition.

During the summer of 1987, Ballard joined a

naval expedition. His older son, Todd, accompanied him. "If I have one regret about having chosen the life of an undersea explorer," he said, "it's the cost to my family. . . . I have been away so much that sometimes my two sons seemed like strangers."[1]

"My being Todd's father had not been easy for either of us," he wrote.[2] The two were able to spend time touring Europe together after the Navy cruise. Ballard looked forward to Todd's joining the crew for the inaugural JASON Project.

That fall Ballard's book *The Discovery of the Titanic* hit the best-seller lists. A few months later the children's version, *Exploring the Titanic*, sold many thousands of copies. People could not learn enough about the fabled ship.

Ballard's research ship set sail for the Mediterranean Sea in June 1988. Todd Ballard, a high school senior, joined the crew as an *Argo* "flyer." Robert Ballard planned to search the seafloor between Italy and North Africa for interesting JASON Project exploration sites. Very soon, they discovered a new, active underwater volcano, Marsili Seamount. The next summer it would be the focus of the geology portion of JASON Project I.

Archeology would be JASON's second focus. Ballard's experience exploring shipwrecks had widened his interest to include exploring history under the sea. This section of the Mediterranean was a heavily traveled trade route between Rome and the ancient North African civilizations. Ballard believed it would be rich with wrecks and artifacts, particularly in deeper, colder water. There they would be out of the reach of marauding scuba divers and fishing-trawler nets, well preserved in the icy sea.

But after ten days of searching with *Argo*, only six clay vessels, called amphoras, had been located. They lay in an area called Skerki Bank. Ballard decided to use them as a starting point for a debris field search. Sure enough, they soon found a mass of ancient debris, but no ships.

The next day, Ballard was relaxing with members of the TV crew when Todd rushed in. "We've got her," he yelled. "We've found a ship."[3] The data logger noted a large heap of amphoras. This sounded promising, but when Ballard ordered a second pass over the area, they seemed to have vanished. Almost twenty-four hours passed before they were found. Again, an eager Todd Ballard was present in the control room, though his shift was over. "That's it, we've found her," he shouted.[4]

More than a dozen artifacts lay in such a way that it was clear they had fallen together. "At long last we'd found our shipwreck," Robert Ballard said. He ordered *Argo* raised. "I wanted to leave the area largely unexplored so that next year we could give students a chance to participate in the thrill of being scientific explorers."[5]

From the Mediterranean, they sailed into the Atlantic, some six hundred miles west of France. Ballard's undersea quarry was the *Bismarck*, the most notorious battleship in Hitler's navy. Four British warships had witnessed her sinking. At the time of World War II, more than thirty years had passed since the *Titanic* went down. Yet less-than-perfect celestial navigation was still being used to gauge position at sea. Each Royal Navy ship gave different coordinates of longitude and latitude for the *Bismarck*. The search area that resulted measured more than two hundred square miles, much larger than the *Titanic*'s. Still, Ballard believed that the *Bismarck* would be easy to find.

Sonar showed that the sea bottom was not flat at the site. A steep, underwater mountain divided the search area. One of the sinking positions was on the other side of the mountain from the other three. Ballard realized that the search might be more like "looking for a needle in a haystack at night, in a blizzard, with nothing more than a flashlight."[6]

The search began on July 12. The rugged bottom terrain made mowing the lawn difficult. Ballard tried several different strategies, making the search pattern look crazy on paper. Days passed, with no result.

Todd Ballard took the noon-to-4:00 P.M. and midnight-to-4:00 A.M. watches. His father considered him one of the best *Argo* controllers. Todd's greatest hope was for the ship's discovery to come on his watch. He was at *Argo*'s joystick in the small hours of the morning when Robert Ballard noticed discoloration in the seabed, usually a sign of disturbance.

"Switch to down-looking [camera]," he ordered. "Okay, zoom in."

The image on the screen was unclear, but definitely man-made.

"I told you this was the ship," Todd exclaimed.[7]

By 5:00 A.M. the team members were sure they had located an impact crater. But no large pieces of debris had been spotted and nothing identified the

*Oceanographers use a variety of robots and submersibles to explore underwater wrecks. On a real expedition, scientists would use just one of these underwater vessels at a time.*

site conclusively as the *Bismarck*'s. Yet it lay only 1,860 yards from the sinking position marked by H.M.S. *Rodney*. After a nine-day search, Ballard dared to hope the warship had been located. That is, until he returned to Woods Hole. When the color slides taken by *Argo*'s still camera were developed, Ballard viewed them alone in his office.

"Click: another piece of nondescript wreckage," he remembered. "Click: a twisted ribbon of metal. . . . Click: a beautifully preserved wooden rudder."

Wait, he thought, *Bismarck* did not have a wooden rudder. This debris must have come from a nineteenth-century sailing schooner, he realized. "I felt like someone had driven a stake into my heart."[8]

In life, the *Bismarck* had eluded the entire British Navy for a time. In death, she eluded Ballard. But "I'm an eternal optimist," he said. "Whenever something bad happens to me, I always say 'What have I learned?'"[9] Like the British, Ballard would hunt the *Bismarck* again.

The following spring, JASON Project I debuted. Ballard's geological and archeological expedition to the Mediterranean would be broadcast live to schoolchildren. Students would view scientists at work on a movie screen surrounded by a replica of the shipboard control van. Kids could ask questions of Ballard and his colleagues. Twelve museums would host the production. A dress rehearsal was held on April 26, 1989, with museum staff in the audience.

"Dr. Ballard, we have you on screen. All museums have signed on. Countdown to air: 5, 4, 3, 2, 1." The voice came via satellite from Turner Broadcasting in Atlanta, Georgia.

"Good morning from the Mediterranean," Ballard responded from Marsili Seamount. "You've tuned in just in time to see a live launch of *Hugo* and *Jason*."[10]

The *Jason* robot was ready to explore at last. Ballard's idea of robotic telepresence, first envisioned in 1980, had become real nine years later. *Jason* would not be tethered to *Alvin*, however, as *JJ* had been. Instead, a new vehicle, *Hugo* (or huge *Argo*), would be towed by the research ship. *Jason* would be tethered to *Hugo*.

As Ballard watched on a video monitor, *Hugo*, with *Jason* inside, entered the rough seas. Museum workers all over America watched along with him. Suddenly, everyone's screens went blank. Ballard realized immediately what had happened. With an anguished cry, he snatched off his headphones and ran from the control room.[11]

The ship had descended from an enormous wave. The next swell jerked it back up too quickly for *Hugo*'s tow cable to handle the strain. The cable snapped. *Hugo* and *Jason*, millions of dollars' worth of Ballard's vision, plunged to the bottom of the sea. How could the show go on?

Luckily, Ballard had brought a small backup vehicle, nicknamed *Medea* after the mythical enchantress who helped *Jason*. Even more fortunately, *Hugo*'s sonar still worked perfectly after the plunge. Ballard's team located the sunken vehicles and used *Medea* to haul them to the surface for repair. His dedicated technicians even had them ready to go when live broadcasts to children began May 1.

For the next five days, thousands of students witnessed the discovery of hydrothermal vents by the JASON Project. No one had guessed that they existed in the Mediterranean Sea. Students saw *Jason* dart between tall sulfide chimneys and avoid the shimmering, superheated water shooting out of them.

The next week, at Skerki Bank, broadcast attention turned from geology to archeology. Students across the country watched as *Medea*'s cameras revealed a heap of ancient amphoras and other artifacts.

"We're here! All right!" a crew member hollered.

The crew's whoops and whistles were transmitted live to America.

"You just saw how professional we are when we make our discoveries," Ballard laughingly told the audience.

Dr. Anna McCann, an underwater archeologist, spoke more seriously. "Just imagine, you are seeing what no one has seen for two thousand years."[12]

Led by Dr. McCann, the JASON Project retrieved and carefully preserved dozens of ancient pots, tools, and kitchen utensils for study by experts. Their most significant find was a gold coin that dated the shipwreck to approximately A.D. 355. Dr. McCann suggested that the wreck be called the *Isis* after the Egyptian goddess who watched over sailors.

The live broadcasts were a grand success. More than two hundred fifty thousand students had experienced the thrill of exploration and discovery live. "[It was] one of the most intense and satisfying experiences of my life," said Ballard.[13]

Ballard and his team sailed from this triumph to their second pursuit of the *Bismarck*. Todd Ballard joined the expedition. Initially the search seemed as hopeless as the one in 1988. "After seven days . . . [everyone was] going crazy with the close quarters and the numbing routine of life at sea. . . . My troops were beginning to wonder if I had led them on a wild goose chase," Robert Ballard remembered.[14]

Father and son watched the sunset together that evening. "Maybe the *Bismarck* has disappeared into a black hole," Robert Ballard joked. "I'm beginning to wonder if we're ever going to find it."

"Don't worry, Dad," Todd reassured him. "You always do."[15]

That night, Robert Ballard's Trivial Pursuit quiz match was interrupted with welcome news. Old, reliable *Argo* was being used for the search. Its cameras showed quantities of man-made material and a greatly disturbed bottom. Mud and rocks tumbled in swirled piles. It was an underwater landslide, Ballard realized. "Only one thing could have caused an avalanche this big—the *Bismarck*."[16]

For two days, a parade of debris, even an enormous upside-down gun turret, flew by. But where was the main wreck? An exhausted Ballard watched the search from a video monitor in his cabin. Finally, he spotted another turret on the screen. Two gun barrels were still attached. It was part of a massive white shape. His triumphant shout could be heard clear across the ship. It was the *Bismarck*.

The crew crowded into the control van for a celebration. Todd Ballard had again hoped to be on watch when the discovery was made. "How much did our shift miss it by, Dad?" he asked.

"About thirty meters," his father replied. Apparently, *Argo* had just missed the main wreck more than once. "I could see Todd's disappointment, mixed with pride and elation," Ballard remembered.[17]

Just as had happened on the *Titanic* expedition, Ballard's mood changed quickly. The tension of the search was replaced by a feeling of sadness. He remembered the many young sailors on both sides of the battle who had died there.

Only three days remained to document the wreck site. *Argo*'s camera crossed and recrossed *Bismarck*'s decks. Ballard was especially proud that Todd controlled *Argo* during some of the most dangerous and demanding sweeps.[18]

Many areas of the ship were beautifully preserved. British bombardment had destroyed others. Strange black lines appeared repeatedly on the deck. Only after several passes did Ballard realize they formed a Nazi swastika.

Ballard held a memorial service for the dead from the *Bismarck* and H.M.S. *Hood* before the cruise ended on June 12, 1989. A rope wreath made by one of the crew was committed to the water. Ballard remembered a moment of silence broken only by "the wind, the throbbing of the ship's engines and the cry of seabirds."[19] He was particularly moved to think that

*In 1989, more than forty years after the sinking of the* Bismarck, *above, Ballard and his crew discovered the remains of the most notorious battleship in Hitler's navy.*

many of the lost sailors had been no older than his son Todd, who stood nearby, listening quietly.

After several weeks spent publicizing the discovery, Ballard retreated with his family to their vacation home in the Montana mountains. He planned several weeks of fishing and water-skiing with his sons. But while he was gone for a brief business trip, Todd left too. He drove across the country to see his girlfriend in Massachusetts.

Several nights later, the Ballards were awakened by a sheriff's deputy's knock. "Dr. Ballard," the pale-faced young man said, "I'm sorry to tell you that your son is dead."[20] Todd had been driving too fast on a narrow Cape Cod road in the rain. He missed a curve and crashed into a tree.

"When I closed my eyes," Ballard wrote, "I saw Todd clearly again, his face pulsing with excitement as he leaned over the *Argo* flyer station." His son's death was the cruelest pain he had ever faced.[21] Ballard dedicated his book *The Discovery of the Bismarck* to Todd. He wrote, "To my son Todd, who like so many young men aboard the *Bismarck* and the *Hood*, died just as the glow of manhood was beginning to burn bright."[22]

# Jason and His Argonauts

In the painful period after Todd's death, Robert and Marjorie Ballard separated. Robert Ballard spent the remainder of 1989 working at sea on Navy projects. He gave much thought to his marriage and decided to ask for a divorce. It was finalized the next year.

Ballard rededicated himself to his work, particularly the JASON Project. In May 1990, the JASON Project team sent the *Jason* ROV to the bottom of Lake Ontario, between the United States and Canada. The robot explored the wrecks of two naval vessels from the War of 1812, the *Hamilton* and the *Scourge*. Students gathered in fourteen museums to view *Jason*'s findings live over satellite transmission.

That year students could pilot the *Jason* robot in

real time. As a student manipulated a joystick at a museum site, *Jason* received its signals via satellite. The student could actually guide *Jason* around the wreck.

Selected students visited Ballard's control barge on Lake Ontario. They viewed computer images of the sunken ships. The lake's cold, fresh water preserved the vessels beautifully. *Jason*'s three independent sonar systems transmitted signals that computers turned into detailed 3-D pictures. "The [video] pictures were muddy," one student noticed, "but computers removed the dirt."[1]

That year Ballard renewed his longtime association with the National Geographic Society. He served as host of its television show *National Geographic Explorer*. He needed some coaching for this new role as TV personality. So he sought the advice of Barbara Earle, who had served as National Geographic's link to the JASON Project. She was an experienced television producer. Ballard and Barbara Earle fell in love. They married on January 12, 1991.

The Ballards became partners in business as well as in life. They formed a company, Odyssey Corporation, to produce television specials for National Geographic and other outlets. For their first project, they decided to film Robert Ballard's exploration of ships sunk in the World War II battle for Guadalcanal. So many vessels, Allied and Japanese, were destroyed there it became known as Iron Bottom Sound. Ballard flew to the South Pacific to make a preliminary sonar survey of the area that summer.

Then disaster struck JASON Project III in the

Galápagos Islands in December 1991. Two weeks before broadcasts were to begin, a barge carrying equipment sank in nine thousand feet of water. One item lost was *Jason Junior*, the little robot that had descended the *Titanic*'s grand staircase. Children who had come to regard the robot as a friend were saddened by the loss.

Friends of the JASON Project rallied to provide replacement equipment in record time. "It was an incredible response by so many different people [who] had bought into JASON and didn't want it to perish," Ballard remembered.[2] He told reporters at the time, "Scientific exploration and discovery is full of surprises and setbacks. To me, the fact that we are able to go forward with our broadcast shows scientific teamwork at its best."[3] All broadcasts to students went ahead on schedule.

Ballard flew back to Guadalcanal in July 1992. His wife accompanied him as film producer. The U.S. Navy was partially funding the expedition to commemorate the battle's fiftieth anniversary and lent Ballard its submersible *Sea Cliff* and ROV *Scorpio*. The Ballards' film would document the three phases of the battle, highlighting ships engaged in each phase. But the two ships in which Ballard was most interested—the *Canberra* and the *Quincy*—had not turned up in the 1991 preliminary survey.

Ballard's team began mowing the lawn with its ROV. On the very first pass, *Canberra* appeared. "There she was, large as life on the sonar screen. Don't ask me how we could have missed her in 1991," Ballard said.[4] Equipment problems dogged them throughout the expedition. "When one of our two vehicles [*Sea Cliff* and *Scorpio*] was working, the other one always seemed to need fixing."[5]

Luckily, *Quincy* was found a few days later. Ballard, with a Navy pilot and a National Geographic photographer, dove in *Sea Cliff* to the wreck. For the final time, Ballard would cheat death in a submersible. The team hit bottom at only three thousand feet, far shallower than the *Titanic* or *Bismarck* sites. The pilot and copilot Ballard went through their routine checks. Ballard noted that the carbon dioxide meter showed a level far higher than it should. As he reported this to the pilot, the needle jumped into the danger zone. The system used to clean the air inside the submersible had malfunctioned. Carbon dioxide was not being "scrubbed" out by a filter. Every time the men exhaled, the deadly gas their lungs produced was poisoning the air.

The pilot calmly double-checked the reading and changed the filter. The meter reading remained the same. The pilot dropped the descent weights and began a high-speed ascent. "Donning EBS (emergency breathing systems)," he reported to the shipboard controller.[6] Ballard immediately flashed back to the fire he survived on *Archimede* in 1973. He placed the breathing mask on his face. Fifty minutes would be required to reach the surface. Just then, the photographer cried out. The intake-outlet hoses had broken loose from his face mask. The three men would now have to share the two working masks. While taking turns breathing clean air, they had to remain calm and repair the broken mask. This life-or-death

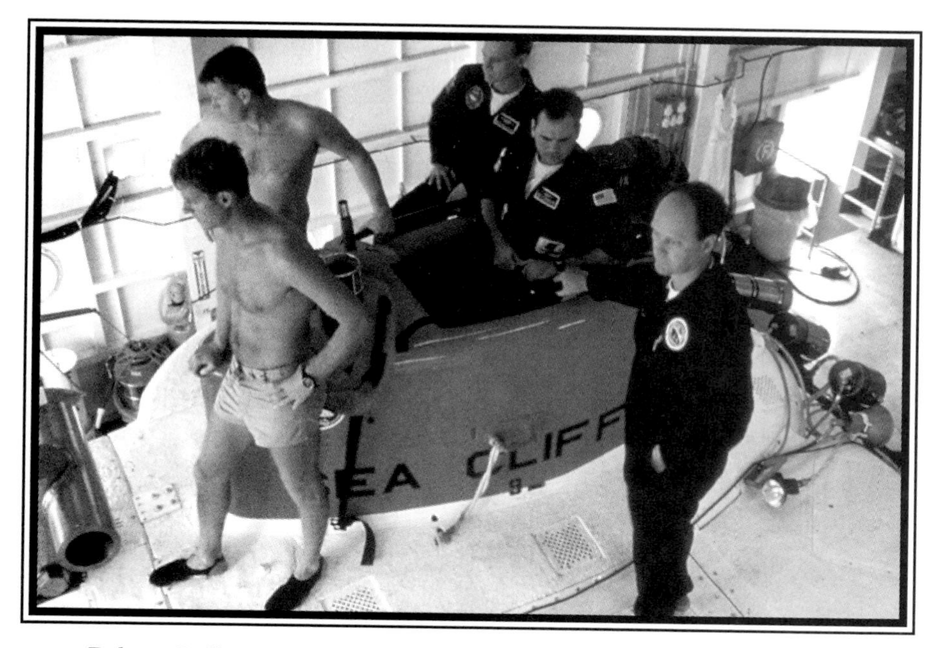


*Robert Ballard, right front, with the U.S. Navy submersible* Sea Cliff *and its crew. The Navy lent* Sea Cliff *to Ballard for his exploration of Iron Bottom Sound in 1992.*

maneuver was being watched above on video by the surface team. It "probably looked like a Three Stooges slapstick routine," Ballard said.[7] Happily, they repaired the mask and rose safely. Just that morning Ballard had told his wife that he was probably getting too old for such shenanigans in submersibles.[8]

The expedition succeeded in identifying and filming eleven ships. The Ballards' film proved very popular as a National Geographic television special.

JASON Project IV in 1993 returned to the scene of one of Ballard's greatest scientific achievements. Students viewed the tube worms and black smokers of Baja California's hydrothermal vents. Again students piloted *Jason* as it explored a field of rare, mushroom-shaped vents. A new component had been added that year. Scientists on land also participated by telepresence, designing experiments and piloting *Jason* remotely to perform them. In the two years since the Galápagos disaster, the JASON Project had rebounded and grown. Now there were twenty-five transmission downlinks, including sites in four different countries.

The *Lusitania* was Ballard's quarry for the next television special that he and his wife produced for National Geographic. This famed ocean liner was sunk by a torpedo fired from a German submarine in World War I. The sinking shocked the world because the rules of war prohibited attacking civilian vessels. *Lusitania*'s position, in shallow water in sight of the southern coast of Ireland, was well known.

Ballard's team dived to the hulk in the submersible *Delta* and used two ROVs. They produced a

*Ballard looks small next to this giant propeller salvaged from the wreck of the* Lusitania. *The luxury ocean liner was torpedoed by a German submarine during World War I.*

3-D computer picture of the mangled remains. Broken and bent like a boomerang, the *Lusitania* had lost everything above the deck, including the four smokestacks. Worst of all, it was draped with dozens of fishing nets that were dangerous to Ballard's submersible. On one dive, *Delta* was immobilized when its propeller sucked in a nylon net. Fortunately, the submersible was able to drop its tail section and escape.

Mystery had surrounded the sinking because many eyewitnesses reported hearing two explosions. The German submarine claimed to have fired only once. Many suspected that the civilian liner had illegally carried munitions, which then blew up. Ballard's exploration disproved this theory. Instead, he speculated, it was most likely that combustible coal dust in the nearly empty storage area had ignited as a result of the torpedo.

Barbara Ballard was pregnant during this adventure. After three years of marriage, the Ballards had their first child. William Benjamin Aymar Ballard was born in January 1994. "Our life together was clearly heading off in a new direction," Ballard said.[9]

Only a month later, Ballard left for the rain forests of Belize in Central America. JASON Project V highlighted tropical ecosystems and the coral reefs of the Caribbean coast.

Ballard's life was rich and full. But it seemed to be going in so many directions. He began to search again for a defining vision to unite his interests. Would he find it?

11

# Mystic and Beyond

Two very different events of the early nineties caused a new vision to form in Ballard's creative brain. The success of the first five JASON Projects confirmed the value of telepresence as an educational tool. And the stripping of artifacts from the *Titanic* by a commercial venture, R.M.S. *Titanic*, Inc., enraged him. "I so disagree with what they do, I don't even like to talk about it," he declared.[1]

It was all so unnecessary, he believed. "As we saw people salvaging the *Titanic* . . . and actually destroying the site, we saw the need to educate the public that they didn't need to do that," Ballard said.[2] The salvagers justified the removal of artifacts by displaying them in museums. But what if, Ballard reasoned, telepresence enabled museumgoers to view the actual artifacts up close, in real time, while they lay undisturbed at the bottom of the sea? What if a museum exhibit used virtual reality to simulate the experience of being inside the *Titanic* almost thirteen thousand feet down? What if everyone could see what Ballard had seen, thrill to what had thrilled him?

In 1994, the governor of Connecticut, Lowell Weicker, invited Ballard to his office. Ballard had been involved in projects with the Sea Research Foundation in Mystic, Connecticut, for more than a year. Governor Weicker asked Ballard to move his base of operations to Mystic permanently. Ballard said that he envisioned an Institute for Exploration, the first museum to focus on the deep sea. It would be interactive. It would use cutting-edge technology to make museumgoers feel as close to scientific explorers as possible. An adjoining research center would become Ballard's headquarters. His efforts with the Odyssey Corporation and the JASON Project would move to Connecticut as well. In addition, the research center would be the country's premier facility for the new field of deepwater archeology, which Ballard and JASON Project I had done so much to promote. The governor liked the idea.

"Connecticut Plan Luring Finder of *Titanic*," a *Boston Globe* headline read. "My interests have changed," Ballard stated. "Mystic is the perfect setting for those interests."[3] Shortly before Governor Weicker announced their proposal, Ballard notified Woods Hole that he would retire in 1997. The new museum's funding passed the Connecticut state legislature in December 1994.

The year 1995 was rich in adventure for Ballard. He led four major expeditions in only seven months. JASON Project VI in February focused on the big island of Hawaii. Student and teacher argonauts captured venomous spiders and killer caterpillars from the Hawaiian rain forest. They performed chemical experiments on lava flows and volcanic gases. Though the expedition took proper safety precautions, danger dogged their work. The soles of the argonauts' boots smoked on newly deposited lava. Half a million students in five countries tuned in for JASON VI.

Shortly thereafter, Ballard borrowed the Navy's *NR-1*, its smallest nuclear submarine, to dive to the wreck of the *Andrea Doria*. One of the last great transatlantic liners, she collided with another ship and sank in 1956. The site was only 250 feet deep, southwest of Nantucket Island in Massachusetts.

Ballard fulfilled his agreement with the Navy to land safely on a sunken hull. Then he fulfilled his own mission. Ballard now actively sought a wreck to serve as his underwater museum. *Lusitania* was already a possible candidate. Would *Andrea Doria* join the list? Ballard did a preliminary survey of the fishnet-draped wreck.

In 1995, Ballard published his autobiography, *Explorations: My Quest for Adventure and Discovery Under the Sea*. In the book, he looked back to find meaning in his action-packed career. Ballard compared his life to the epic voyages of the mythical Greek heroes like Jason. Like them, he dreamed. Then he prepared and assembled his crew. Voyaging forth and being tested came next. Finally, he overcame and gained truth. He also wrote movingly about his son Todd's struggle to find a place for himself in the shadow of a famous father. Many reviewers praised the book, which became a best-seller.

In August, Ballard mounted his first expedition under the banner of the new Institute for Exploration. He undertook an extensive survey of the floor of the Mediterranean Sea. Using *NR-1*, his team stayed submerged for days at a time, working intensely. They produced a detailed underwater map of ancient trade routes between Africa and Rome. *NR-1*'s exceptionally powerful sonar allowed them to scrutinize more than a hundred square miles of artifact-rich territory. The result "would take archeologists a lifetime to take advantage of," Ballard boasted.[4]

From the Central Mediterranean, Ballard sailed for the Greek island of Kea. There, in 1916, the *Titanic*'s sister ship *Britannic* sank while serving as a floating hospital. *NR-1* and two ROVs enabled Ballard to do a complete survey of the wreck. Though broken in two, *Britannic* had survived in excellent condition, with both pieces side by side. This delighted Ballard.[5] Had he found his ideal underwater museum site? "*Britannic* is really an excellent candidate," he admitted.[6]

JASON Project VII debuted on the Internet in 1996 with an exploration off the coast of Florida. Kids with home computers followed divers off Key Largo as they explored coral reefs and encountered sharks, dolphins, and manatees. Thousands of children around the world signed the online guest book, thanking Ballard.

A journalist visiting JASON Project VII observed Ballard for a morning of shipboard television broadcasts. "In the entire time . . . I did not see him in one place for more than five minutes," the journalist marveled.[7] Viewing scientists at work over the Internet amazed the journalist. "Seeing [a diver] under the water with the bubble helmet on, talking to me and students dialing in from everywhere—it blew my mind," he told Ballard.[8]

The next year Ballard retired from Woods Hole, his professional home of thirty years. It was not to be a restful retirement. At age fifty-five he worked harder than ever. The Ballard family moved from Massachusetts to Connecticut, and Ballard shifted his center of operations to Mystic. There he would create the Institute for Exploration at Mystic Aquarium. Ballard also continued his deep-sea explorations.

"Journey from the Center of the Earth," JASON Project VIII, zeroed in on two of Earth's unique environments. Iceland and Yellowstone National Park in Wyoming showed off their geysers and hot springs to worldwide audiences. Again, the Internet played a prominent role.

Armed with the map he created two years earlier, Ballard returned to the Mediterranean in June 1997. Dr. Anna McCann, his colleague on the first JASON expedition, joined him. *NR-1* immediately found a wreck every other day or so. The scientists had their hands full and called a halt. "We realized we had found a graveyard of ships spanning 2,000 years," Ballard said.[9] The oldest dated from about 100 B.C., making it one of the oldest ships ever found.

*The Institute for Exploration is the first museum to focus on the deep sea. From his headquarters here in Mystic, Connecticut, Ballard continues to plan future ocean expeditions.*

The expedition proved that deep-sea archeology had emerged as a revolutionary new science. Previous archeologists, confined to the top two hundred feet of the sea, believed ancient sailors rarely ventured into open waters. Now they knew better. Ancient history must be rewritten, McCann said.[10]

*NR-1*'s large grappling arm removed the heaviest artifacts, such as big lead anchors. Trustworthy old *Jason* continued to serve Ballard well. Its smaller mechanical arms retrieved delicate pieces like glassware. "You come in with your robot, this most advanced technology on the planet, almost like a spaceship, and you're hovering over a picture of antiquity two [thousand years] old," Ballard said. "It's a breathtaking, unbelievable scene."[11]

In December 1997, Emily Rose Ballard was born. After three boys, having a girl thrilled Ballard. "She's the happiest, most good-natured spirit I've ever met in my life," he said.[12] Four-year-old Benjamin was a whirlwind of a boy. "He wants to be an astronaut. He wants to be an explorer. He's got the genes, that's for sure," his father reported.[13] Grown-up brother Douglas had graduated from college. He managed a large health/fitness facility and saw his dad frequently.

The same month the *Titanic* roared back into Ballard's life. James Cameron's Oscar-winning film appeared in theaters. It soon became the top-grossing movie of all time and sparked interest in all things *Titanic*. Ballard's book *The Discovery of the Titanic* shot back onto the best-seller list. Interviewers clamored for his opinion of the film. "I loved it," he said.[14]

The three levels of the ocean—coastal, middle, and

deep—formed the focus of JASON Project IX in 1998. The most ambitious project yet, it spanned three expeditions over four months.

The Institute for Exploration (IFE) opened its first public exhibits in May. But Ballard was not present. Near Midway Island, far out in the Pacific, he searched for the remains of the aircraft carrier *Yorktown*. A casualty of the Battle of Midway, a turning point of World War II, it lay somewhere almost a mile deeper than the *Titanic*. Ballard hoped to locate and film the wreck in time for the fifty-sixth anniversary of the sinking on June 4. Thousands of people, including many survivors of the battle, avidly followed the expedition's progress daily on the National Geographic Web site.

Eighteen fruitless days passed. On May 20, Ballard watched video images transmitted by the Navy's Advanced Tethered Vehicle, a state-of-the-art ROV. *Yorktown* veteran Bill Surgi watched with him. A length of chain appeared on the monitor. "There's something," Surgi said.[15] His words eerily repeated those of *Argo* flyer Stu Harris when he had first spotted the *Titanic*'s debris.[16] Ballard had triumphed again. *Yorktown* was found.

♦ ♦ ♦

Today, Ballard continues to maintain a hectic daily pace. He still juggles several roles in his professional life. "[I've] shifted away from natural history to human history and shifted more back into exploration, more high-risk exploration," he explains.[17] He continues to

*The World War II aircraft carrier* Yorktown *in action. The photograph was taken from a fighter plane, whose wing is visible in the foreground. The wreck of the* Yorktown *lay hidden on the bottom of the sea for more than half a century—until Robert Ballard decided to find it.*

head the JASON Project and serve as president of the Institute for Exploration.

Ballard has booked expeditions for the year 2000 and has plans for others in 2001, when he will be nearing sixty years of age. His 1999 projects include archeological expeditions to the Black Sea, between Turkey and Russia, and a return to the Mediterranean. The year 1999 also marked the opening of IFE's Challenge of the Deep exhibit. This exciting experiment in virtual reality is designed to make museumgoers feel as if they were in the ocean's depths themselves.

Ballard laughs when he says that kids have asked him "to stop looking for things so there's something left for them. I want them to know that we've just looked at a smidgen of the world. . . . [They need] to understand [that] the game is not over, it's just begun. That ocean exploration is in its infancy."[18]

He remains in the thick of the game himself.

# Chronology

1942—Robert Duane Ballard born in Wichita, Kansas, on June 30.

1948—Moves to San Diego, California.

1953—Moves to Downey, California.

1959—Becomes trainee at Scripps Institution of Oceanography.

1960—Graduates from Downey High School.

1965—Receives bachelor of science degree from University of California, Santa Barbara.

1966—Doctoral student at University of Hawaii; marries Marjorie Hargas.

1967—Transfers to University of Southern California; assigned to Woods Hole Oceanographic Institution (WHOI) as scientific liaison officer for United States Navy.

1968—Son Todd born.

1969—Leaves U.S. Navy and becomes a research associate in ocean engineering at WHOI.

1970—Son Douglas born.

1973—Phase one of Project FAMOUS.

1974—Receives Ph.D. from University of Rhode Island; phase two of Project FAMOUS.

1975—First article published in *National Geographic*.

1976—Cayman Trough expedition.

1977—Galápagos Rift expedition; discovery of hydrothermal vents; meets Bill Tantum, president of the *Titanic* Historical Society.

1978—East Pacific Rise expedition to Baja California.

1979—Second Galápagos Rift expedition; second East Pacific Rise expedition; discovery of "black smokers."

1980—Sabbatical year in Palo Alto, California; envisions ocean exploration by telepresence; rival *Titanic* expedition mounted by Jack Grimm.

1981—Returns to Woods Hole; second Grimm expedition.

1982—Founds the Deep Submergence Laboratory at Woods Hole.

1983—Publishes his first book, *Exploring Our Living Planet*; final Grimm expedition.

1984—Exploration of *Thresher* wreck site.

1985—Finds the *Titanic*.

1986—Second *Titanic* expedition; first use of remotely operated vehicle (ROV).

1987—Publishes best-seller, *The Discovery of the Titanic*.

1988—Preliminary cruise of JASON Project; first *Bismarck* expedition.

1989—JASON Project I cruises to Marsili Seamount and Skerki Bank; finds the *Bismarck*; death of Todd Ballard.

1990—JASON II, Lake Ontario; Robert and Marjorie Ballard divorce.

1991—Marries Barbara Earle; JASON III, Galápagos.

1992—Expedition to Iron Bottom Sound (Guadalcanal).

1993—*Lusitania* expedition; JASON IV, Sea of Cortez.

1994—William Benjamin Ballard born; JASON V, Belize; funding voted for Institute for Exploration.

1995—Autobiography, *Explorations: My Quest for Adventure and Discovery Under the Sea,* is published; JASON VI, Hawaii; *Britannic* expedition.

1996—JASON VII, Florida.

1997—Retires from Woods Hole Oceanographic Institution; JASON VIII, Iceland and Yellowstone; Emily Rose Ballard born.

1998—JASON IX, Monterey-Bermuda-Sea of Cortez; *Yorktown* expedition; Institute for Exploration opens in Mystic, Connecticut.

1999—IFE's Challenge of the Deep exhibit opens.

# Glossary

***Alvin***—Three-person submarine used for research and exploration of the deep sea by Woods Hole Oceanographic Institution.

**ANGUS**—Still-camera sled towed by cable from a research vessel to explore the deep sea. Photographs must be developed after the sled comes to the surface.

***Argo***—Video camera sled towed by cable from a research vessel to explore the deep sea. Video images are immediately visible on shipboard monitors. May also hold still cameras and other equipment.

**black smokers**—Hollow sulfide chimneys found at hydrothermal vents that belch water hot enough to melt lead.

**chemosynthesis**—Use of chemicals called sulfides as food.

**Deep Submergence Laboratory**—Engineering and design center at Woods Hole Oceanographic Institution, founded by Robert Ballard to invent and develop instruments for deep-sea exploration.

***Hugo***—Huge *Argo*, a deep-towed garage for *Jason*. Abandoned during JASON Project I.

**hydrothermal vents**—Underwater hot springs. Sulfide-rich oases of life in the deep ocean.

**IFREMER**—French governmental agency for oceanography.

**Institute for Exploration (IFE)**—Museum and research institute for deep-sea archeology founded by Robert Ballard in Mystic, Connecticut.

***Jason***—Unmanned ROV, a robot with video cameras and its own motor for exploring the deep sea.

***Jason Junior (JJ)***—Experimental *Jason* used to film inside the *Titanic*.

**JASON Project**—Educational foundation started by Robert Ballard to promote science education and bring live research and exploration into the classroom via telepresence.

***Medea***—Backup vehicle used after *Hugo* was abandoned during JASON Project I.

**Mid-Atlantic Rift**—Underwater mountain range in the middle of the Atlantic Ocean where new seafloor is being created from underground lava flows.

**mowing the lawn**—Doing an ocean search by following parallel lines that slightly overlap.

***NR-1***—The U.S. Navy's smallest nuclear submarine. Frequently lent to Ballard in the nineties.

**Odyssey Corporation**—Company founded by Robert and Barbara Ballard to organize and film deep-sea expeditions.

**Project FAMOUS**—Joint French-American study of the Mid-Atlantic Rift, undertaken in the early seventies.

**ROV (remotely operated vehicle)**—Robot used in place of humans by scientists and technicians for research and exploration.

**sonar**—Instrument using sound waves to locate and identify underwater objects.

**submersible**—Small, manned submarine, used primarily for research and exploration.

**telepresence**—Doing research and exploration by using robots. Scientists and students watch video or online images and manipulate the robot in real time.

**Woods Hole Oceanographic Institution (WHOI)**—Private research center for oceanography located in Woods Hole, Massachusetts.

# Chapter Notes

## Chapter 1. *Titanic* Found

1. Don Lynch, *Titanic: An Illustrated History* (New York: Hyperion, 1992), p. 33.

2. Robert Ballard, *Exploring the Titanic* (New York: Scholastic, 1988), p. 16.

3. Robert Ballard, *The Discovery of the Titanic* (New York: Warner, 1987), p. 61.

4. Ibid., p. 80.

5. Ibid.

6. Ibid.

7. Ibid., p. 81.

8. *Secrets of the Titanic*, National Geographic Video, 1986.

9. Frederic Golden, "A Man With Titanic Vision," *Discover*, January 1987, p. 60.

10. *Secrets of the Titanic* video.

11. Robert Ballard, *Explorations: My Quest for Adventure and Discovery Under the Sea* (New York: Hyperion, 1995), p. 266.

12. Ibid.

13. *Secrets of the Titanic* video.

14. Ibid.

15. Ballard, *The Discovery of the Titanic*, p. 84.

16. Ibid.

## Chapter 2. Boyhood by the Sea

1. Douglas Colligan, "Titanic Robots: Robert Ballard Interview," *Omni*, July 1986, p. 64.

2. Charles Pellegrino, *Her Name: Titanic* (New York: Avon, 1988), p. 56.

3. Ibid., p. 41.

4. Mark Henricks, "Deep Sea Detective," *Boys' Life*, August 1994, p. 29.

5. "Underwater Explorer: Interview with Dr. Robert Ballard," *Nova Online*, 1997, <http://www.pbs.org/wgbh/nova/titanic/ballard.html> (April 30, 1997).

6. Colligan, p. 73.

7. Doug Garr, "The Real Captain Nemo," *Reader's Digest*, April 1992, p. 174.

8. Colligan, p. 66.

9. *Nova Online* interview.

10. Garr, p. 174.

11. Pellegrino, p. 42.

12. Ibid.

### Chapter 3. Young Scientist

1. Michael Fremont, "Interview With Robert Ballard," *Internet Roundtable*, August 2, 1995, <http://jasonproject.org/JASON/HTML/PEOPLE_ballard_interview_people_html> (April 26, 1997).

2. Charles Pellegrino, *Her Name: Titanic* (New York: Avon, 1988), p. 44.

3. Ibid., p. 45.

4. Frederic Golden, "A Man With Titanic Vision," *Discover*, January 1987, p. 56.

5. Robert Ballard, *Explorations: My Quest for Adventure and Discovery Under the Sea* (New York: Hyperion, 1995), p. 23.

6. Douglas Colligan, "Titanic Robots: Robert Ballard Interview," *Omni*, July 1986, p. 66.

7. Pellegrino, pp. 47–48.

8. Ballard, p. 26.

9. Ibid., p. 30.

10. Ibid., p. 38.

11. Ibid., p. 39.

12. Ibid.

13. Victoria A. Kaharl, *Water Baby, the Story of Alvin* (New York: Oxford University Press, 1990), p. 128.

14. Ballard, p. 100.

15. Robert Ballard, *The Discovery of the Titanic* (New York: Warner, 1987), p. 34.

## Chapter 4. Puzzle of the Continents

1. Mark Henricks, "Deep Sea Detective," *Boys' Life*, August 1994, p. 28.

2. Ibid.

3. Robert Ballard, "Project FAMOUS II—Dive Into the Great Rift," *National Geographic*, May 1975, p. 605.

4. Ibid., p. 604.

5. Victoria A. Kaharl, *Water Baby, the Story of Alvin* (New York: Oxford University Press, 1990), p. 165.

6. Ballard, p. 615.

7. Doug Garr, "The Real Captain Nemo," *Reader's Digest*, April 1992, p. 177.

## Chapter 5. Mysteries of the Deep

1. Robert Ballard, *Explorations: My Quest for Adventure and Discovery Under the Sea* (New York: Hyperion, 1995), p. 158.

2. Ibid., p. 174.

3. Ibid., p. 180.

4. Ibid., p. 181.

5. Victoria A. Kaharl, *Water Baby, the Story of Alvin* (New York: Oxford University Press, 1990), p. 173.

6. Ballard, p. 184.

7. Kaharl, p. 173.

8. Douglas Colligan, "Titanic Robots: Robert Ballard Interview," *Omni*, July 1986, p. 64.

9. Ballard, p. 188.

10. Robert Ballard, *Exploring Our Living Planet* (Washington, D.C.: National Geographic Society, 1983), p. 123.

11. Ballard, *Explorations*, p. 191.

12. Ballard, *Exploring Our Living Planet*, p. 131.

13. Ballard, *Explorations*, pp. 188–189.

14. Michael Fremont, "Interview With Robert Ballard," *Internet Roundtable*, August 2, 1995, <http://jasonproject.org/JASON/HTML/PEOPLE_ballard_interview_people_html> (April 26, 1997).

15. Ballard, *Explorations*, p. 189.

## Chapter 6. The Door Swings Open

1. Robert Ballard, *The Discovery of the Titanic* (New York: Warner, 1987), p. 37.

2. Joseph Cone, *Fire Under the Sea* (New York: William Morrow, 1991), pp. 226–227.

3. Robert Ballard, *Explorations: My Quest for Adventure and Discovery Under the Sea* (New York: Hyperion, 1995), p. 203.

4. Frederic Golden, "A Man With Titanic Vision," *Discover*, January 1987, p. 58.

5. Ballard, *Explorations*, p. 221.

6. Ibid., p. 223.

7. Ibid., p. 236.

8. Ibid., p. 13.

## Chapter 7. A Night to Remember

1. Walter Lord, *A Night to Remember* (New York: Amereon House, 1955), p. 14.

2. Don Lynch, *Titanic: An Illustrated History* (New York: Hyperion, 1992), p. 85.

3. Robert Ballard, *Exploring the Titanic* (New York: Scholastic, 1988), p. 21.

4. *Titanic*, A&E Home Video, 1994.

5. Ibid.

6. Ballard, p. 23.

7. *Titanic* video.

8. Lord, p. 65.

9. Ibid., p. 138.

10. *Titanic* video.

11. Ballard, p. 25.

12. *Titanic* video.

13. Lynch, p. 118.

14. Lord, p. 68.

15. Jennifer Kirkpatrick, "I Survived the Titanic," *National Geographic World*, June 1996, p. 27.

16. *Titanic* video.

17. Lynch, p. 126.

18. *Titanic* video.

19. Lord, p. 89.

20. Walter Lord, *The Night Lives On!* (New York: Morrow, 1986), p. 227.

21. Ballard, p. 29.

22. *Titanic* video.

23. Lynch, p. 150.

24. Lord, *A Night to Remember*, p. 148.

25. Lord, *The Night Lives On!*, p. 160.

26. *Titanic* video.

27. Ibid.

## Chapter 8. Titanic Hero

1. Charles Pellegrino, *Her Name: Titanic* (New York: Avon, 1988), p. 106.

2. Robert Ballard, *The Discovery of the Titanic* (New York: Warner, 1987), p. 87.

3. Ibid., p. 89.

4. Ibid., p. 90.

5. Ibid.

6. Ibid.

7. Ibid., pp. 90–91.

8. Frederick Golden, "A Man With Titanic Vision," *Discover*, January 1987, p. 61.

9. Ballard, p. 94.

10. Douglas Colligan, "Titanic Robots: Robert Ballard Interview," *Omni*, July 1986, p. 80.

11. Robert Ballard, *Exploring the Titanic* (New York: Scholastic, 1988), p. 37.

12. Ballard, *The Discovery of the Titanic*, p. 101.

13. Pellegrino, p. 126.

14. Ibid., p. 133.

15. Colligan, p. 79.

16. Ballard, *Exploring the Titanic*, p. 47.

17. Ibid., p. 40.

18. Robert Ballard, *Explorations: My Quest for Adventure and Discovery Under the Sea* (New York: Hyperion, 1995), p. 297.

19. Ballard, *Exploring the Titanic*, p. 41.

20. Ballard, *The Discovery of the Titanic*, p. 114.

21. Victoria A. Kaharl, *Water Baby, the Story of Alvin* (New York: Oxford University Press, 1990), p. 290.

22. Ballard, *The Discovery of the Titanic*, p. 119.

23. Ibid., p. 131.

24. Kaharl, p. 292.

25. Ibid.

26. Ballard, *The Discovery of the Titanic*, p. 134.

27. Kaharl, p. 293.

**Chapter 9. History Under the Sea**

1. Robert Ballard, *The Discovery of the Bismarck* (New York: Warner, 1990), p. 44.

2. Robert Ballard, *Explorations: My Quest for Adventure and Discovery Under the Sea* (New York: Hyperion, 1995), p. 363.

3. Robert Ballard, *The Lost Wreck of the Isis* (New York: Scholastic, 1990), p. 18.

4. Ibid., p. 19.

5. Ibid.

6. Robert Ballard, *Exploring the Bismarck* (New York: Scholastic, 1991), p. 43.

7. Ballard, *The Discovery of the Bismarck*, p. 51.

8. Ibid., p. 55.

9. Doug Garr, "The Real Captain Nemo," *Reader's Digest*, April 1992, p. 178.

10. Ballard, *The Lost Wreck of the Isis*, p. 28.

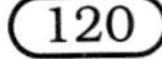

11. Ibid.

12. Ibid., p. 50.

13. Ballard, *The Discovery of the Bismarck*, p. 147.

14. Ballard, *Exploring the Bismarck*, p. 46.

15. Ibid.

16. Ibid., p. 48.

17. Ibid., p. 49.

18. Ballard, *Explorations*, p. 381.

19. Ballard, *Exploring the Bismarck*, p. 59.

20. Ballard, *Explorations*, p. 383.

21. Ibid., p. 384.

22. Ballard, *The Discovery of the Bismarck*, p. 4.

## Chapter 10. Jason and His Argonauts

1. "Water Work: The 1990 Jason Project," *National Geographic*, March 1991, p. 19.

2. Personal interview with Robert Ballard, June 8, 1998.

3. David L. Chandler, "Jason Broadcasts, Minus Jason, Provide a View of the Galápagos," *Boston Globe*, December 5, 1991, p. 52.

4. Robert Ballard, *The Lost Ships of Guadalcanal* (New York: Warner, 1993), p. 72.

5. Ibid.

6. Robert Ballard, *Explorations: My Quest for Adventure and Discovery Under the Sea* (New York: Hyperion, 1995), p. 393.

7. Ibid., p. 394.

8. Ibid.

9. Ibid., p. 405.

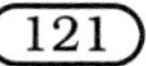

## Chapter 11. Mystic and Beyond

1. Michael Fremont, "Interview with Robert Ballard," *Internet Roundtable*, August 2, 1995, <http://jasonproject.org/JASON/HTML/PEOPLE_ballard_roundtable_interview.html> (April 26, 1997).

2. Personal interview with Robert Ballard, June 8, 1998.

3. "Bay State May Lose Undersea Treasures; Conn. Plan Luring Finder of *Titanic*," *Boston Globe*, October 11, 1994, p. 28.

4. William J. Broad, "Secret Sub to Scan Sea Floor for Roman Wrecks," *The New York Times*, February 7, 1995, p. C9.

5. Robert Ballard, *Lost Liners* (New York: Hyperion, 1997), p. 138.

6. Personal interview with Robert Ballard.

7. L. de Lemos, "An Interview with Doctor Robert Ballard: The Man in Front of the Camera for JASON," *VCN Views*, 1996, <http://views.vcn.net/03/noframes/interviews/ballard.html> (April 29, 1997).

8. Ibid.

9. John N. Wilford, "Roman Ships Found Off Sicily; New Sites Broaden Study," *The New York Times*, July 31, 1997, p. A3.

10. Ibid.

11. Emmy Kondo, "8 Ancient Ships Discovered," *ABCnews.com.world*, July 30, 1997, <http://www.abcnews.go.com/sections/world/shipwrecks730/index.html> (January 12, 1999).

12. Personal interview with Robert Ballard.

13. Ibid.

14. "Titanic the Movie—December 24, 1997," *CNN Transcript: Larry King Live* <http://www.cnn.com/TRANSCRIPTS/9712/24/lkl.00.html> (April 29, 1997).

15. Tom Allen, "8 A.M. local, 0700 May 20 Zulu," May 20, 1998, <http://www. nationalgeographic.com/features/98/midway/dispatches_519.html> (January 12, 1999).

16. Robert Ballard, *Explorations: My Quest for Adventure and Discovery Under the Sea* (New York: Hyperion, 1995), p. 264.

17. Personal interview with Robert Ballard.

18. Ibid.

# Further Reading


Archbold, Rick. *Deep-Sea Explorer: The Story of Robert Ballard, Discoverer of the Titanic*. Boston: Houghton Mifflin, 1996.

Ballard, Robert. *The Discovery of the Bismarck: Germany's Greatest Battleship Surrenders Her Secrets*. New York: Warner, 1990.

——— with Rick Archbold. *The Discovery of the Titanic*. New York: Warner, 1987.

——— with Malcolm McConnell. *Explorations: My Quest for Adventure and Discovery Under the Sea*. New York: Hyperion, 1995.

——— with Rick Archbold. *Exploring the Bismarck*. New York: Scholastic, 1993.

——— with Spencer Dunmore. *Exploring the Lusitania: Probing the Mysteries of the Sinking That Changed History*. New York: Warner, 1995.

———. *Exploring the Titanic*. New York: Scholastic, 1988.

——— and Rick Archbold. *Ghost Liners: Exploring the World's Greatest Lost Ships*. Boston: Little, Brown, 1998.

———. *Lost Liners: From the Titanic to the Andrea Doria*. New York: Hyperion, 1997.

———. *The Lost Ships of Guadalcanal*. New York: Warner, 1993.

———. *The Lost Wreck of the Isis*. New York: Scholastic, 1990.

Lord, Walter. *A Night to Remember*. New York: Bantam, 1955.

Lynch, Don. *Titanic: An Illustrated History*. New York: Hyperion, 1992.

MacQuitty, Miranda. *Ocean*. New York: Knopf Books for Young Readers, 1995.

## Videocassettes

*Secrets of the Titanic*, National Geographic Video, 1986.

*Titanic*, A&E Home Video, 1994.

## Internet Addresses

**The JASON Project**
<http://www.jasonproject.org>

**The Hall of Science & Exploration—Robert Ballard Interview**
<http://www.achievement.org/autodoc/page/bal0int-1>

**The Institute for Exploration**
<http://www.ife.org>

**The *Titanic* Historical Society**
<http://www.titanic1.org>

**Woods Hole Oceanographic Institution**
<http://www.whoi.edu>

# Index

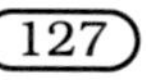